# Readers Theatre
## for
# American History

# Readers Theatre
# for
# American History

Anthony D. Fredericks

2001
Teacher Ideas Press
A Division of
Libraries Unlimited, Inc.
Englewood, Colorado

TEACHER IDEAS PRESS
A Division of
Libraries Unlimited, Inc.
P.O. Box 6633
Englewood, CO 80155-6633
1-800-237-6124
www.lu.com/tip

**Library of Congress Cataloging-in-Publication Data**

Fredericks, Anthony D.
    Readers theatre for American history / Anthony D. Fredericks.
        p. cm.
    Includes bibliographical references.
    ISBN 1-56308-860-6 (pbk.)
    1. Readers' theater. 2. Drama in education. 3. Young adult drama, American. 4. United States--History--Study and teaching (Middle school)--Activity programs.  I. Title.

PN2081.R4 F744 2001
808.5'4--dc21
                                                                00-053689

# Contents

## PART 1
## North America
### Land and Early People

## PART 2
## The Beginnings
## of a New Nation
### The 1600s and 1700s

## PART 3
## The Nation Changes
### The 19th Century

## PART 4
## New Directions
### The 20th Century

## PART 5
## Recent History,
## Recent Challenges
### The 20th and 21st Centuries

# PREFACE

In my conversations with students throughout the past 30 years I've found it interesting that most students' definitions and conceptions of history are repeatedly mundane and lackluster. Too many students (elementary, secondary, and college) perceive history as nothing more than a collection of meaningless facts, dates, people, and places—often isolated and frequently unrelated. Memorizing factual information and regurgitating it on an exam or quiz seems (at least to many students) to be the crux of the entire social studies program or history curriculum.

Yet, history (specifically, American history) is a subject that is vibrant, alive, and dynamic. It achieves potency because it is a part of who we are today and who we will become tomorrow. It is a mosaic of our culture, a tapestry of our heritage, and a portrait of our dreams. It is not the facts that are important, but rather the concepts that weave those facts together into vibrant understandings and colorful perceptions. Memorizing facts is meaningless and irrelevant; helping students acquire an intellectual framework for dealing with relationships and constructing generalizations should always be a major part of history education.

In the last few years social studies education has undergone some remarkable transformations. New standards issued by the National Council for the Social Studies, fresh new trade books written by some of this country's most exciting authors, mind-boggling new Web sites, and a reconfiguration of social studies curricula across the country show the transformations taking place. In many ways, social studies education is now a "hands-on, minds-on" subject in which students take active roles in the learning process. This activity-based approach provides elementary students with a plethora of opportunities to live and experience social studies in purposeful projects and designs.

This book offers a participatory approach to American history education that says when students are provided meaningful opportunities to make an investment of self in their education, that education will become both relevant and dynamic. *Readers Theatre for American History* presents readers theatre scripts that stimulate children to become active participants in selected historical events. Students will work alongside Father Junipero Serra at Mission San Juan Capistrano, they'll stand alongside Thomas Jefferson as he drafts the Declaration of Independence, they'll travel with a brave and determined family as they trek across the Oregon Trail, and they will travel with Neal Armstrong in his history-making trip to the Moon. In short, students will take on the personae of selected historical figures, participate in significant events, and get a "you are there" perspective on the unfolding of critical milestones, memorable circumstances, and colorful venues that have shaped the American experience.

Within these pages is a dynamic variety of creative learning possibilities for your intermediate level classroom (Grades 4–8). Here, your students will discover an exciting cornucopia of mind-expanding and concept-building experiences that will reshape their perceptions of what American history is as well as what it can be. Readers theatre offers opportunities to make history come alive. So, be prepared for lots of action, lots of drama, and lots of fun! Let the adventure begin!

—Tony Fredericks

# Introduction

## The Magic of Storytelling

Not too long ago a colleague asked me what I enjoyed most about teaching children. My response was immediate and emphatic—storytelling! To watch the gleam of excitement in students' eyes while sharing a new book, to observe the look of recognition when presenting a familiar tale, or to see kids' faces light up when embellishing a piece of literature or timeless tale are professional "perks" that go far beyond pay checks and long vacations. I suppose part of my belief that storytelling is the quintessential classroom activity lies in the fact that it is an opportunity to bring life, vitality, and substance to the two-dimensional letters and words on a printed page. So too is it an interpersonal activity—a "never-fail" way to connect with minds and souls and hearts. After more than 30 years of teaching, I never tire of sharing a story with a group of youngsters—it is part of my *raison d'etre* as I hope it will be for them.

The magic of storytelling has been a tradition of every culture and civilization since the dawn of language. It binds human beings and celebrates their heritage as no other language art can. It is part and parcel of the human experience because it underscores the values and experiences we cherish as well as those we seek to share with each other. Nowhere is this more important than in today's classroom. Students who have been bombarded with visual messages (i.e., television) since birth still relish and appreciate the power and majesty of a story well told. Even adults, in their hustle and bustle lifestyles, always enjoy the magic of a story or the enchantment of a storyteller. Perhaps it is a natural part of who we are that stories command our attention and help us appreciate the values, ideas, and traditions we hold dear. So too should students have those same experiences and those same pleasures.

Storytelling conjures up all sorts of visions and possibilities—far away lands, magnificent adventures, enchanted princes, beautiful princesses, evil wizards and wicked witches, a few dragons and demons, a couple of castles and cottages, perhaps a mysterious forest or two, and certainly tales of mystery, intrigue, and adventure. These are stories of tradition and timelessness, tales that enchant, mystify, and excite through a marvelous weaving of characters, settings, and plots, tales that have stood the test of time. These are stories of our youth, stories of our heritage, and stories that continue to enrapture audiences with their delightful blending of good over evil, patience over greed, and right over might. Our senses are stimulated, our mental images are energized, and our experiences are fortified through the magic of storytelling.

## What Is Readers Theatre?

Readers theatre is a storytelling device that stimulates the imagination and promotes *all* of the language arts. Simply stated, it is an oral interpretation of a piece of literature read in a dramatic style. My good friend, Suzanne Barchers, who is also an author of several readers theatre books, states that ". . . the primary focus in readers theatre is on an effective reading of the script rather than on a . . . memorized presentation. . . . The ease of incorporating readers theatre into the language arts program offers teachers an exciting way to enhance that program, especially in today's classrooms that emphasize a variety of reading and listening experiences." (Barchers, 1993).

Simply put, readers theatre is an act of involvement, an opportunity to share, a time to creatively interact with others, and a personal interpretation of what can be or could be. In fact, readers theatre holds the promise of helping children understand and appreciate the richness of language, the interpretation of that language, and how language can be a powerful vehicle for the comprehension and appreciation of different forms of literature. Readers theatre provides numerous opportunities for youngsters to make stories and literature come alive and pulsate with their own unique brand of perception and vision. In so doing, literature becomes personal and reflective—children have a breadth of opportunities to be authentic users of language.

## Students As Storytellers

One of the positive consequences of regular storytelling times in the classroom is that children begin to understand that storytelling is a natural act of communication. Witness the excitement of primary-level students returning from a trip or holiday vacation as they eagerly share their stories with the teacher or other members of the class. Here, the energy level is at an all-time high as family episodes, tales, and personal experiences are shared back and forth. Indeed, youngsters soon learn that we are all storytellers—all with something to share.

When children are provided with regular opportunities in the classroom to become storytellers, they develop a personal stake in the literature shared. They also begin to cultivate personal interpretations of that literature—interpretations that lead to higher levels of appreciation and comprehension. Practicing and performing stories is an involvement endeavor—one that demonstrates and uses numerous language activities. So too do youngsters learn to listen to their classmates and appreciate a variety of presentations.

# What Is the Value of Readers Theatre?

I like to think of readers theatre as a way to interpret historical events without the constraints of skills, memorization, or artificial structures (e.g., props, costumes, elaborate staging, etc.). Readers theatre allows children to breathe life and substance into history—an interpretation that is neither right nor wrong because it will be colored by kids' unique perspectives, experiences, and vision. It is, in fact, the readers' interpretation of an event that is intrinsically more valuable than some predetermined and/or preordained "translation" (something that might be found in a teacher's manual or curriculum guide, for example).

With that in mind, I'd like to share with you some of the many values I see in readers theatre:

- It stimulates curiosity and enthusiasm for history. It allows children to experience history in a supportive and non-threatening format that underscores their active involvement.

- It allows children many different interpretations of the same story and facilitates the development of critical and creative thinking. There is no such thing as a right or wrong interpretation of a story; readers theatre validates that assumption.

- It focuses on all of the language arts—reading, writing, speaking, and listening. It supports a holistic philosophy of instruction and allows children to become responsible learners—ones who seek out answers to their own self-initiated inquiries.

- Because it is the performance that drives readers theatre, children are given more opportunities to invest themselves and their personalities into the production. The same story may be subject to several different presentations depending on the group or the individual students involved. As such, children learn that readers theatre can be explored in a host of ways.

- Children are given numerous opportunities to learn about the major features of selected historical events. This is particularly true when they are provided with opportunities to design and construct their own readers theatre scripts and have unlimited opportunities to discover the wide variations that can be used with a single piece.

- It is a participatory event. The characters as well as the audience are intimately involved in the design, structure, and delivery of the story. As such, children begin to realize that learning history is not a solitary activity, but one that can be shared and discussed with others.

- It is informal and relaxed and does not require elaborate props, scenery, or costumes. It can be set up in any classroom or library. It does not require large sums of money to "make it happen," and it can be "put on" in any kind of environment—formal or informal.

- It stimulates the imagination and the creation of visual images. When children are provided with opportunities to create their own mental images, their comprehension and appreciation of a piece of writing will be enhanced considerably. Because only a modicum of formal props and "set up" are required for any readers theatre production, the participants and audience are encouraged to create supplemental "props" in their minds—props that may be more elaborate and exquisite than those found in the most lavish of plays.

- It enhances the development of cooperative learning strategies by requiring children to work together toward a common goal and supporting their efforts in doing so. Readers theatre is not a competitive activity, but rather a cooperative one in which children share, discuss, and band together for the good of the production.

- It is valuable for non-English speaking children or non-fluent readers. Readers theatre provides them with positive models of language usage and interpretation that extend far beyond the "decoding" of printed materials. It allows them to see "language in action" and the various ways in which language can be used.

- Teachers and librarians have discovered that readers theatre is an excellent way in which to enhance the development of communication skills. Voice projection, intonation, inflection, and pronunciation skills are all promoted within and throughout any readers theatre production. Children who need assistance in these areas are provided with a support structure that encourages the development of necessary abilities.

- It facilitates the development and enhancement of self concept. Because children are working in concert with other children in a supportive atmosphere, their self-esteem mushrooms accordingly. Again, the emphasis is on the presentation, not necessarily the performers. As such, students have opportunities to develop levels of self-confidence and self-assurance that would not normally be available in more traditional class productions.

- It enhances creative and critical thinking. Children are active participants in the interpretation and delivery of a story; as such, they develop thinking skills that are divergent rather than convergent and interpretive skills that are supported rather than directed.

- When children are provided with opportunities to write and/or script their own readers theatre, their writing abilities are supported and encouraged. As children become familiar with the design and format of readers theatre scripts, they can begin to use their own creative talents in designing their own scripts and stories.

- It is fun! Children of all ages have delighted in using readers theatre for many years. It is stimulating, encouraging and fascinating, relevant and personal. Indeed, try as I might, I have not been able to locate a single instance (or group of children) in which (or for whom) readers theatre would not be an appropriate learning activity. It is a strategy filled with a cornucopia of possibilities and promises.

## Presentation Suggestions

It is important to remember that there is no single way to present readers theatre. What follows are some ideas you and the children with whom you work may wish to keep in mind as you put on the productions in this book. Different classes and even different groups of children within the same class will have their own methods and modes of presentation; in other words, no two presentations may ever be the same. However, here are some suggestions that will help make any readers theatre performance successful.

### *Preparing Scripts*

One of the advantages of using readers theatre in the classroom is the lack of extra work or preparation time necessary to get "up and running." By using the scripts in this book, your preparation time is minimal.

- After a script has been selected for presentation, make sufficient copies. A copy of the script should be provided for each actor. In addition, two or three extra copies (one for you and "replacement" copies for scripts that are accidently damaged or lost) is also a good idea. Copies for the audience are unnecessary and are not suggested.

- Each script can be bound between two sheets of colored construction paper or poster board. Bound scripts tend to formalize the presentation a little and lend an air of professionalism to the actors.

- Highlight each character's speaking parts with different color highlighter pens. This helps kids track their parts without being distracted by the dialogue of others.

## Starting Out

Introducing the concept of readers theatre to your students for the first time may be as simple as sharing a script with the entire class and "walking" them through the design and delivery of that script.

- Emphasize that a readers theatre performance does not require any memorization of the script. It's the interpretation and performance that count.

- You may wish to read through an entire script aloud taking on the various roles. Let students know how easy and comfortable this process is.

- Encourage selected volunteers to read assigned parts of a sample script to the entire class. Readers should stand or sit in a circle so that other classmates can observe them.

- Provide opportunities for additional re-readings using other volunteers. Plan time to discuss the ease of presentation and the different interpretations offered by different readers.

- Readers should have an opportunity to practice their script before presenting it to an audience. Take some time to discuss voice intonation, facial gestures, body movements, and other features that could be used to enhance the presentation.

- Allow children the opportunity to suggest their own modifications, adaptations, or interpretations of the script. They will undoubtedly be "in tune" with the interests and perceptions of their peers and can offer some distinctive and personal interpretations.

- Encourage students to select non-stereotypical roles within any readers theatre script. For example, boys can take on female roles, and girls can take on male roles; the smallest person in the class can take on the role of a giant, and a shy student can take on the role of a boastful, bragging character. Provide sufficient opportunities for students to expand and extend their appreciation of readers theatre through a variety of "out of character" roles.

## Staging

Staging involves the physical location of the readers as well as any necessary movements. Unlike a more formal play, the movements are often minimal. The emphasis is more on presentation, less on action.

- For most presentations, readers will stand and/or sit on stools or chairs. The physical location of each reader has been indicated for each of the scripts in this book.

- The position of each reader is determined by "power of character" (Dixon, et al., 1996). This means that the main character is downstage center (in the middle front of the staging area) and the lesser characters are stage right, stage left, or further upstage (toward the rear of the staging area).

- If there are many characters in the presentation, it may be advantageous to have characters in the rear (upstage) standing while those in the front (downstage) are placed on stools or chairs. This ensures that the audience will both see and hear each actor.

- Usually all of the characters will be on stage throughout the entire presentation. For most presentations it is not necessary to have characters enter and exit. If you place the characters on stools, they can face the audience when they are involved in a particular scene and then turn around whenever they are not involved in a scene.

- You may wish to make simple hand-lettered signs with the name of each character. Loop a piece of string or yarn through each sign and hang it around the neck of each character. That way, the audience will know the identity of each character throughout the presentation.

- Slightly more formalized presentations will have characters entering and exiting at various times throughout the presentation. These directions are indicated in the scripts in this book.

- Each reader will have her or his own copy of the script in a paper cover (see above). If possible, use a music stand for each reader's script (this allows readers to use their hands for dramatic interpretations as necessary).

- Several presentations have a narrator to set up the story. The narrator serves to establish the place and time of the story for the audience so that the characters can "jump into" their parts from the beginning of the story. Typically, the narrator is separated from the other "actors" and can be identified by a simple sign.

- As students become more comfortable with readers theatre, invite them to suggest alternative positions for characters in a script. The placements indicated in these scripts are only suggestions; students may want to "experiment" with various staging possibilities. This becomes a worthwhile cooperative activity and demonstrates the variety of interpretations possible with any single script.

## *Props*

Two of the positive features of readers theatre are the ease of preparation and the ease of presentation. Informality is a hallmark of any readers theatre script.

- Much of the setting for a story should take place in the audience's mind. Elaborate scenery is not necessary—simple props are often the best. For example:

    — A branch or potted plant can serve as a tree.

    — A drawing on the chalkboard can illustrate a building.

    — A hand-lettered sign can designate one part of the staging area as a particular scene (e.g., swamp, castle, field, forest).

    — Children's toys can be used for uncomplicated props (e.g., telephone, vehicles, etc.).

    — A sheet of aluminum foil or a remnant of blue cloth can be used to simulate a lake or pond.

- Costumes for the actors are unnecessary. A few simple items may be suggested by students. For example:

    — Hats, scarves, or aprons can be used by major characters.

    — A paper cutout can serve as a tie, button, or badge.

    — Old clothing (borrowed from parents) can be used as warranted.

- Some teachers and librarians have discovered that the addition of appropriate music or sound effects can enhance a readers theatre presentation. For example, the ringing of a bell after the signing of the Declaration of Independence; the "clip-clopping" of two coconut halves on a wooden board to simulate the sound of hoofbeats (during a trip on the Oregon Trail); the sound of rock and roll music in the background of a script about the 1980s.

- It's important to remember that the emphasis in readers theatre is on the reading—not on any accompanying "features." The best presentations are often the simplest.

## *Delivery*

I've often found it advantageous to let students know that the only difference between a readers theatre presentation and a movie role is the fact that they will have a script in their hands. This allows them to focus more on **presenting** a script rather than **memorizing** a script.

- When first introduced to readers theatre, students often have a tendency to "read into" their scripts. Encourage students to look up from their scripts and interact with other characters or the audience as necessary.

- Practicing the script beforehand can eliminate the problem of students burying their heads in the pages. In so doing, children understand the need to involve the audience as much as possible in the development of the story.

- Voice projection and delivery are important in allowing the audience to understand character actions. The proper mood and intent needs to be established—aspects which are possible when children are familiar and comfortable with each character's "style."

- Children should **not** memorize their lines, but rather should rehearse them sufficiently so that they are "comfortable" with them. Again, the emphasis is on delivery, so be sure to suggest different types of voice (e.g., angry, irritated, calm, frustrated, excited, etc.) that children may wish to use for their particular character(s).

## *Post-Presentation*

As a wise author once said, "The play's the thing." So it is with readers theatre. In other words, the mere act of presenting a readers theatre script is complete in and of itself. It is not necessary, or even required, to do any type of formalized evaluation after readers theatre. Once again, the emphasis is on informality. Readers theatre should and can be a pleasurable and stimulating experience for children.

What follows are a few ideas you may want to share with students. In doing so, you will be providing youngsters with important languaging opportunities that extend and promote all aspects of your social studies or history program.

- After a presentation, discuss with students how the script enhanced or altered the original story.

- Invite students to suggest other characters who could be added to the script.

- Invite students to suggest new or alternate dialogue for various characters.

- Invite students to suggest new or different setting(s) for the script.

- Invite students to talk about their reactions to various characters' expressions, tone of voice, presentations, or dialogues.

- After a presentation, invite youngsters to suggest any modifications or changes needed in the script.

- Invite each of the "cast" members to maintain a "production log" or reading response log in which they record their thoughts and perceptions about the presentation. Encourage them to share their logs with other class members.

Presenting a readers theatre script need not be an elaborate or extensive production. As children become more familiar and polished in using readers theatre they will be able to suggest a multitude of presentation possibilities for future scripts. It is important to help children assume a measure of self-initiated responsibility in the delivery of any readers theatre. In so doing, you will be helping to ensure their personal engagement and active participation in this most valuable of language arts activities.

It is hoped that you and your students will find an abundance of readers theatre scripts in this book for use in your own classroom. But these scripts should also serve as an impetus for the creation of your own classroom or library scripts. By providing opportunities for your children to begin designing their own readers theatre scripts you will be offering them an exciting new arena for the enhancement of their appreciation of history and their "role" in its recreation.

# References

Barchers, Suzanne. *Readers Theatre for Beginning Readers*. Englewood, CO: Teacher Ideas Press, 1993.

Dixon, Neill, Anne Davies, and Colleen Politano. *Learning with Readers Theatre: Building Connections*. Winnipeg, Canada: Peguis Publishers, 1996.

# PART 1

# North America

### Land and Early People

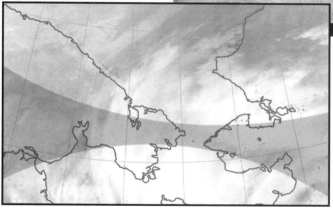

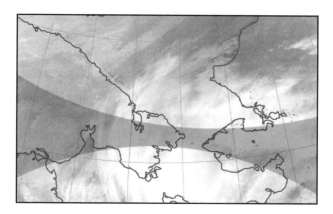

# Across the Bering Strait

## Staging

The narrator sits on a stool or chair at the front of the staging area. The characters (who are designated by letters, rather than names) are seated on the floor in a semicircle.

                          Woman (B)
                              X

        Man (C)                                Woman (D)
            X                                      X

    Man (A)                                            Child (E)
        X                                                  X

                          Narrator
                              X

[Note: For this production the characters are speaking in English. It should be pointed out to students that the first people who came to North America did not speak English. Linguists have postulated that before the time of Columbus, 12 language families and over 200 languages had developed in what is now the United States. We do not know what language these characters would have spoken.]

**NARRATOR:**   There are several theories and varying beliefs about how the first people arrived in what is now the Americas. This particular production is based on current scientific thought, which may or may not be in agreement with Native American beliefs.

The time is about 12,000 years ago in what is now considered the Pleistocene Ice Age. A small group of nomads has been traveling for about 10 months. They have left the land now known as Siberia to cross what is now the Bering Strait. At the time of their crossing this area of the world was solid land connecting Siberia to the current state of Alaska. As we look in on this group, they are huddled around a small fire and talking about the day's activities.

**A:**   This was a good day. We have traveled far and have been very successful in finding game for our group. We will eat well for the next day.

**B:**   Tell us of your hunt. What animals did you see? Where did you go?

**C:**   We walked the way of our ancestors. They, too, walked far in search of the great animals. According to legend, they were able to find many different kinds of animals to kill and feed their people.

**NARRATOR:**   The group of people around this fire has been following the migrations of woolly mammoths, bison, deer, and horses. The paths they use are the same paths used by those animals. They know that as long as they follow the animals, they will have sufficient game to feed their people and supply the necessary materials to clothe and house them.

**A:**   Today we found several mammoths. They are very large so we had to be very careful. Several of us walked very quietly around one of the large beasts. The soft soles of our leather moccasins muffled any sounds that we would make. Each man had in his hand a long spear made from the wood of a young sapling and fitted with a stone that had been hammered into a sharp edge. Each stone had been lashed carefully to the end of a spear.

**E:** Were you scared of the woolly mammoth?

**C:** Yes, we were scared. But we believed that with many men surrounding the beast we would be able to slay it.

**B:** It has been a long time since we have seen one of the mammoths. We have found a few caribou, but finding a mammoth would feed our clan for a long time.

**NARRATOR:** Woolly mammoths are important to the survival of the nomads. The skin of the mammoth provides the wanderers with clothing and various coverings that help protect them from the bitterly cold weather in this part of the world. Bones from the mammoth are used as weapons to help kill other animals. Bones are also used to help build temporary shelters along the way. Stuck in the ground and covered with hides, the bones provide a framework for makeshift shelters. The woolly mammoth is also an important source of food. The meat from a single mammoth can feed a tribe of nomads for many days.

**D:** Tell us more about your hunt today.

**C:** There were 10 of us and we had surrounded a woolly mammoth that was feeding on the tall grass. Quietly, we approached the giant. At a signal from our leader we each threw our spear at the beast. The mammoth made a loud noise and began to run directly at two of the men.

**E:** And then what happened?

**A:** The two men began to run, but the mammoth stumbled. There were eight spears that had found their mark and the animal was losing much blood. He was getting weaker and weaker. We all stayed a distance away from him until he fell to his knees and then on to his side. We approached cautiously as the great beast was dying. It was a long time before we felt safe enough to touch him.

**E:** And, then, what did you do?

**C:**   We each took out a sharp stone that we carry whenever we go on a hunt. We sharpen these stones while gathered around the night campfires. Each is made by chipping one stone with the face of another stone. Small flakes fall from the edges of the first stone. After much time and work the stone becomes sharp and is useful for cutting the meat of a mammoth.

**B:**   The women also use these stones to prepare the meat for cooking. After the men bring in the large slabs of meat, we cut the meat into smaller pieces, which can be placed on sticks and held over the fires for cooking. These stones are important tools for our survival.

**A:**   It took us a long time, but we were able to cut large pieces of meat from the bones of the woolly mammoth. Each one of us placed a slab of meat over our shoulders and began the long walk back to the camp.

**NARRATOR:**   Nomads depended upon the game they found for their survival. If there were a drought, then there may have been few animals along the way. Different species of animals had varying migration patterns; often these were regular and predictable, sometimes they were not. Finding game was more a matter of chance; it was not always easy because often it depended on seasonal weather patterns, the availability of grass or other food sources, or other unpredictable factors.

**D:**   The mammoths are good providers, but we cannot depend on them alone. We have had difficulty in the past finding the herds of these animals. Shouldn't we look for other animals, too?

**A:**   Yes. There are legends from the people who have passed this way before; legends that tell of long periods of time when there were no animals . . . long periods of time when there was no food . . . long periods of time when the weather was cold and bitter. Yes, these legends also tell of time when people died from these conditions, their bones mixing with the bones of the animals they hunted.

**B:** We must be cautious. This is a long journey and we must plan wisely.

**C:** The animals are moving all the time. They, too, are looking for food to sustain them. If we do not find these animals we shall die. If we kill too many of these animals there shall not be enough to provide for us during the remainder of our journey.

**D:** Our journey is not easy. We depend on the wisdom of the animals we seek. They not only guide us, but they also provide for our needs.

**A:** It has been a long day and we must prepare for tomorrow's hunt. We must ready our tools and prepare our weapons.

**C:** Our weapons are few, but they have helped us. The large bones and stones we use help us kill the animals we need. It is time to gather them together.

**B:** Tomorrow shall be another long day. It shall be a day of hunting . . . a day of searching . . . a day of surviving.

**D:** And we shall survive—as our ancestors did and as our children and their children will after us.

**NARRATOR:** The group of people you see behind me represent the thousands of tribes, clans, and families that traveled across the Bering Strait in search of food and game. As time went on, more and more people became part of the "great migration," which according to some scientists, lasted for thousands of years. After about 8500 B.C., Ice Age animals such as mammoths and bison died out (perhaps from climate changes or overhunting). As big-game hunting dwindled, people began to turn to food gathering and, eventually, farming as sources of food. The unnamed people who crossed the Bering Strait endured many hardships during their travels, but their migration set the stage for the development of what we now know as North America.

# Possible Extensions

1. Invite students to develop a time line of the peoples who crossed the Bering Strait. Post a long strip of newsprint along one wall of the classroom and encourage students to post significant events in chronological order along the strip.

2. Invite students to research some of the animals that lived during the time of these migrations. Divide the class into several small groups to research mammoths, camels, horses, caribou, and buffalo.

3. Students can obtain up-to-date information about the land bridge by logging on to http://whyfiles.news.wisc.edu/061polar/anthro.html. Invite students to share this information (orally or in writing) with another class.

4. Invite students to create a readers theatre script about a hunt (for a deer or bison) this group of people may have participated in during their travels.

5. Invite students to gather information (from books or the Internet) on other theories or ideas on how Native Americans arrived in the land we now call the United States. What are some other scientific theories? What are some Native American legends or beliefs about how they arrived? Provide opportunities for students to share and discuss their findings with each other.

# A Day in Mesa Verde

## Staging

The four characters can all be sitting cross-legged on the floor. They should be placed in a circular arrangement around a make-believe campfire (sticks with a few construction paper "flames"). The narrator can be placed at a podium or lectern at the front of the staging area.

Father
X

Mother          ("flames")          Son
X                                     X

Daughter
X

Narrator
X

**NARRATOR:** It is sometime around A.D. 1300 deep in the rock-ribbed country of what will one day become the states of Colorado, Arizona, New Mexico, and Utah. This is a land of contrasts, a land of beauty, and a land of a great and noble people—the Anasazi. The Anasazi were hunter-gatherers, who eventually became farmers. They relied on unpredictable rainfall and a system of irrigation to grow their crops. They also traded with other peoples in the region—the Hohokam and Hopis of Arizona and the Zunis of New Mexico. They also built trails and roads that can be seen to this day.

The Anasazi are best known for their cliff dwellings—elaborate houses and buildings built into the sides of steep rock cliffs. A spectacular example of this type of architecture is Mesa Verde. Mesa Verde is located in what is now the southwestern corner of Colorado. Most of the dwellings, constructed of stone and sun-dried brick called adobe, stretched along the sides of towering cliffs.

**MOTHER:** I am worried, Husband. The rains do not come as frequently as they did in the past.

**SON:** Yes, there is much dryness. It is difficult for us to grow our crops as we once did.

**DAUGHTER:** You are right. In the old days the land was rich and there was much water. Our people were able to grow squash and corn and we were able to store much of it in the kivas for the long winters.

**FATHER:** You are all right. The fields are not full of the foods we need. It is very dry and water is difficult to find. I do not know what we will do. These are very difficult days for us.

**SON:** Tell us, father, how was it in the old days? What was it like?

**FATHER:** It was much different. According to the legends of the Wise Ones, our people were once wanderers. Many thousands of years ago they traveled over this land looking for animals to hunt and roots to dig up. For reasons no one remembers, our ancestors decided to settle on the land and use the land to grow crops. We became farmers and lived in small villages. Most of the houses were built over pits in the ground.

**DAUGHTER:** What else, father? What else was different in those days?

**FATHER:** One of our great weapons was the atlatl, or spear thrower. We used it to propel small spears at animals. It was a very efficient hunting tool. But this tool was replaced by the bow and arrow.

**SON:** Did the people become hunters?

**FATHER:** No, our people still lived from the land. For a long time they farmed corn and squash. But then they discovered beans and those were added to our farms and to our diet. But, I think, our greatest change came when the ancestors began to make pottery. Depending on where a group of people lived, they made a special kind of pottery. Some villages made gray pottery, some made black-on-white pottery, and some groups made redware pottery. This pottery was used to store items and was very valuable when we traded with other villages and with other peoples.

**DAUGHTER:** I don't understand. Why were there so many kinds of pottery?

**MOTHER:** There were different kinds of clay found in different regions. Also, some peoples preferred a special kind of design or manufacturing process.

**SON:** There must have been many changes. Is that right?

**FATHER:** Yes, but you must remember that the changes of which I speak took place over many generations. Perhaps one of the greatest changes was when our people began to live in larger and larger villages. These were villages of many houses, many fire pits, and many buildings. This was the time when the village of which we are now a part, the cliff village of Mesa Verde, was built.

**DAUGHTER:** So, our village of Mesa Verde has not been here since the beginning of time?

**MOTHER:** No, but our people are ancient people. We have been on this land for many, many years. It is here, however, in this sacred place of Mesa Verde, that we built a great village. It is here where our peoples have lived for many centuries. It is here where our peoples have farmed the mesas, river bottoms, plateaus, and canyons with corn and squash and beans. It is here where our great and thriving population settled and prospered. We raised tall towers and built a city of 100 rooms in the sides of the cliffs and caves. We dug great ceremonial pits and raised our children to be strong and proud. We placed our symbols and petroglyphs on the canyon walls to celebrate our gods and legends and to bring us rain and fertility.

**FATHER:** And that is why the decision of the elders is so difficult.

**SON:** What do you mean, Father?

**FATHER:** The elders have decided that we must move. They have decided that the drought that has plagued our land for many years will plague it for many more years. The growing season gets shorter and shorter and we cannot survive if there is not enough water.

**DAUGHTER:** But, we cannot leave. This is our home. This is where we live and where we have become one with the land.

**MOTHER:** Is there no other way?

**FATHER:** I'm afraid not. The elders have made their decision and we must obey.

**SON:** But, I don't want to leave this place. Here is where I grew up. Here is where I learned to hunt the deer and plant the corn that feeds our people. Father, I do not want to leave.

**FATHER:** I understand your concern, my son. But we must listen to the wisdom of the elders. They are the ones who guide and lead our people.

**MOTHER:** But this is not fair. We have been here for many years.

**DAUGHTER:** I am greatly saddened by this turn of events. How can we leave the land we love? How can we leave behind our customs and traditions? Can we not call upon the spirits to help us? What about Kokopelli?

**NARRATOR:**  Kokopelli was both a magician and a Kachina Spirit for the Anasazi. He would travel from village to village playing his magical flute. Images of him can be found everywhere, etched into the red rocks of Mesa Verde and in other villages of the Anasazi.

**SON:**  Yes, cannot Kokopelli protect us now from what is happening? Cannot Kokopelli protect us from the drought that has plagued our land for many years? Cannot Kokopelli save us so that we do not have to move away?

**FATHER:**  Kokopelli has much magic, but I do not know if he has the magic of the rain. I do not know if he can influence the wisdom of the elders. I'm afraid it is too late. The elders have made their decision and neither Kokopelli nor we can change that decision.

**DAUGHTER:**  I do not wish to move.

**MOTHER:**  None of us wants to move, but I'm afraid your father is right. The elders have made their decision. It is a difficult time and they have made a difficult decision. We must obey their commands.

**NARRATOR:**  Mesa Verde was home to the Anasazi Indians for more than 1,000 years. This settlement began during the time of the Roman Empire and lasted until the latter part of the 13th century. For reasons that are not entirely clear to archaeologists, the Anasazi mysteriously abandoned this part of the country leaving ruins of their homes scattered throughout the area. Several theories have been postulated. One of the most interesting is that there was a 30-year drought beginning about 1270 that may have significantly shortened the growing season. A large population of people would have been difficult to feed. Thus, the Anasazi may have left to seek more fertile land for their crops. Whatever the reason, their villages and lifestyle were an important part of Southwestern culture and the early history of this country.

## Possible Extensions

1. If possible, invite students to initiate a small vegetable garden in a corner of the school grounds or at home. Invite them to grow three crops: squash, corn, and beans. What challenges do they experience with each crop? Is one crop easier to grow than another?

2. Invite students to create a readers theatre script about a day in the life of an Anasazi child at Mesa Verde.

3. Invite students to investigate maps of the Four Corners region of the United States. Encourage them to research the various Indian tribes that lived in this region and to plot those settlements on one or more maps.

4. If possible, work with the art teacher to help students construct their own pottery from clay. What challenges do they face? Do they think their pottery would last for hundreds of years as did the Anasazi's?

5. Students may be interested in gathering additional information about the Anasazi from the following Web sites:

   http://seamonkey.ed.asu.edu/~hixson/cuff/Anasazi.html

   http://sipapu.gsu.edu

   http://www.desertusa.com/ind1/du_peo_ana.html

6. Your students may be interested in reading one or more of the following books:

   *Anasazi* by Leonard Everett Fisher (New York: Atheneum, 1997).

   *Cities in the Sand: The Ancient Civilizations of the Southwest* by Scott Warren (San Francisco: Chronicle Books, 1992).

   *Houses of Adobe: Native Dwellings: The Southwest* by Bonnie Shemie (Seattle: Tundra Books, 1995).

   *Indians of the Southwest* by Karen Liptak (New York: Facts on File, 1991).

# Leif Eriksson Discovers Vinland

## Staging

The characters can all be seated on chairs or stools. They should all be facing the same direction (in the direction of the arrow) as they might be on a ship. The narrator can be standing off to the side or can be out of view of the audience.

        X   Thor        X   Leif

◄ - - - - - - - - - - - - X   Olaf        X   Bjarni

        X   Snorri

                                            Narrator
                                              X

**NARRATOR:** Leif Eriksson was the son of the great Viking explorer Eric the Red. Born in Iceland in about A.D. 980, he and his family moved to Greenland two years later. There he grew into a strong and handsome man filled with adventure and wanderlust. He had a strong urge to travel and when he was 19 he sailed for Norway, the homeland of his family.

**15**

There, he met the king and learned about Christianity. After one year he returned to Greenland.

It was in Greenland that he heard about the voyages of another adventurer who had seen a strange new land. Leif couldn't resist. He purchased a ship and got ready to sail for a new land.

In the first scene, we find Leif trying to convince a group of sailors that they should sail with him. This scene takes place on the docks in a small village in Greenland.

## Scene 1

**LEIF:** I am looking for a few sailors who would join me to look for a new land—a new land in a distant place.

**THOR:** What is this land you talk of, Leif?

**LEIF:** It is a land of rich soil and tall trees. It is a land of abundance. It is a land of many plants and many animals.

**OLAF:** Why has no one gone this way before?

**LEIF:** Perhaps they are not the brave adventurers we are. Perhaps they are afraid of the unknown. Maybe they are content to live their simple lives as they always have.

**SNORRI:** You seem to know much about this new land.

**LEIF:** I only know what has been passed down to me by others and by my own reckoning.

**BJARNI:** But, what riches will we find, Leif?

**LEIF:** I hope to find tall trees to use as ships' masts. In our country of Greenland there are no tall trees so we need the timber from other lands.

**THOR:** Do you think we will find riches of another kind?

**LEIF:** I do not know. But we will be patient and see where the winds will take us.

### Scene 2

**NARRATOR:** Leif and his men set out on their long and difficult voyage. The men are not happy with the work and the endless expanse of sea.

**SNORRI:** Day after day there is nothing but sky and ocean. I am growing weary of such sights.

**OLAF:** Perhaps young Snorri complains too much. I fear he has not been on many voyages across the ocean. Perhaps he should have stayed in the safety of the harbor, in the safety of the village.

**SNORRI:** I am as brave as you, Olaf. It's just that there is an endless expanse of ocean before us. This is an ocean that few have sailed, that few have seen. I'm just not sure what we will find.

**THOR:** I, too, am sick and tired of day after day of nothing but water. And the food! The food is barely edible. I do not know how much longer I can go on eating the same biscuits and dried meat.

**BJARNI:** Not only is the food tough, so is the work. We trim the sails, clean the rudder, and remove water from the bilge day after day after day. The routine never changes; it is always the same.

**OLAF:** I am not sure that our friend Leif knows exactly where he is going. He seems to be headed towards the west, but I'm still not sure he knows what's out there.

### Scene 3

**NARRATOR:** After many days the men sight land and put ashore. But because the land is barren and full of rocks, they set sail again. After several more days they sight another land, this time with white sandy beaches. They land on this new place and explore it. After a few days they leave and are sailing southward.

LEIF:   We have seen some new places. But we still haven't found the land we are looking for.

BJARNI:   (*excitedly*) Look ahead, friends, there is a new land before us.

SNORRI:   You are right, my friend. The land you see is covered with green and it stretches beyond our sight.

LEIF:   Then, it is here we will land. Put out the small boats and let us explore this new and inviting place.

## Scene 4

NARRATOR:   Leif and his men disembark from their ship and begin to explore the new land. It is much different from the others lands they have seen on their voyage.

OLAF:   Is this the rich land you spoke of, Leif?

LEIF:   (*excitedly*) It is certainly a land of riches. Look, there are endless fields of self-sown wheat. The hills are covered with great expanses of tall trees. And, everywhere you look there are sweet wild grapes—grapes for eating and grapes for wine.

THOR:   This is indeed a rich land. What shall we call it?

LEIF:   Look at this land. The soil is dark and rich and shall be perfect for growing crops. The rivers and streams are overflowing with fish to fill both our storage sheds and our bellies. This is a land that has much to offer. I believe we should call it Vinland: the land of wine.

## Scene 5

NARRATOR:   Soon after their arrival on Vinland, Leif and his men set about to build shelters for the winter.

SNORRI:   How long will we stay here Leif?

**LEIF:** We will stay here through the winter. Then, we must sail back to Greenland and tell our people of this rich and great land.

**OLAF:** Surely, they will not believe what we have found here. Surely no one would believe what we have found here. This land is unlike any other we have seen.

**LEIF:** You are right, Olaf. This is a land of promise and opportunity . . . a land where people can settle, raise families, and live off the richness that is all around. We shall journey back to Greenland in the spring and tell of this land. Perhaps others will come after us to partake of this richness. Families will settle here, homes will be built, and villages will be constructed. The fields will be plowed and planted. The rivers and streams will provide their rich bounty of fish for all to eat. Yes, my friends, this is indeed a land of great possibilities.

**SNORRI:** I hope you are right, Leif. I hope you are right.

## Possible Extensions

1. Invite students to create their own readers theatre script about another voyage of Leif Eriksson that took him further down the eastern coast of what is now North America where he actually set foot in what is now the United States.

2. After performing this script and the one that follows, divide the class into two groups. Invite the groups to engage in a healthy debate on who should be given credit for the discovery of North America: Leif Eriksson or Christopher Columbus.

3. Invite students to draft a petition or write a letter to the editor of the local paper concerning the lack of a Leif Eriksson Day in this country. Why do we celebrate Columbus Day, but not Eriksson Day?

4. Students may be interested in searching for some additional information on Leif Eriksson. The following Web sites can be instructive:

   http://viking.no/e/people/leif/e-leiv.htm

   http://home.rmci.net/khwmd/

5.  Students may be interested in learning more about the Vikings, their discoveries, and their way of life. The following Web sites have lots of information on Vikings:

    http://www.mariner.org/age/vikingexp.html

    http://viking.no/e/life/efood.htm

6.  Your students may be interested in reading one or more of the following books:

    *How Would You Survive As a Viking* by Jacqueline Morley (New York: Watts, 1995).

    *Read About Vikings* by Stewart Ross (Brookfield, CT: Millbrook Press, 2000).

    *The Viking Explorers* by Rebecca Stefoff (New York: Chelsea House, 1993).

    *The Viking News* by Rachel Wright (Cambridge, MA: Candlewick Press, 1998).

    *The Vikings* (Footsteps in Time) by Ruth Thompson (New York: Children's Press, 1998).

# Columbus Pleads His Case

## Staging

The narrator can sit on a stool or stand at a lectern on the side of the staging area. Christopher Columbus should be standing or can move back and forth across the staging area. The other two characters can sit side by side on stools or chairs.

<table>
<tr><td></td><td></td><td>Queen Isabella<br>X</td><td>King Ferdinand<br>X</td></tr>
<tr><td></td><td>Christopher Columbus<br>X</td><td></td><td></td></tr>
<tr><td>Narrator<br>X</td><td></td><td></td><td></td></tr>
</table>

**NARRATOR:** It is spring 1492. For seven years Christopher Columbus has been pleading with King Ferdinand and Queen Isabella of Spain for men and ships to search for a new sea route to the West Indies. He is frustrated because he cannot convince Spain's rulers that the route would bring them riches and their country fame.

21

**QUEEN
ISABELLA:** Christopher, for seven years you have been telling us about this new route to the West Indies. Why should we invest our money and men in something that everyone says can't be done?

**CHRISTOPHER
COLUMBUS:** (*frustrated*) But, dear Queen, it can be done! Even some of the most renowned men of science agree that the world cannot be flat. Most of the scholars of our day believe that the world is round. Look at the work of Juan Carlos who keeps describing the "disappearing horizon" — a horizon that is never reached, but keeps moving away from the traveler. Although there are many who still believe that the earth is flat, the best minds in Europe know that that is just not so.

**KING
FERDINAND:** You are quite passionate about your views. That is all well and good. But, you have asked us for vast sums to finance this voyage into the unknown . . . a voyage across an ocean no one has ever sailed. What will we gain?

**CHRISTOPHER
COLUMBUS:** (*somewhat excited*) Great riches! New lands! New territories! Spices, silk, wealth, and untold fortunes!

**QUEEN
ISABELLA:** (*indignantly*) You sound like a prophet, promising much, but delivering little.

**CHRISTOPHER
COLUMBUS:** (*pleading*) Trust me, my queen. If I discover this new route by sailing west across the Atlantic Ocean your coffers will be filled with gold. Your cabinets will be filled with the finest spices. Your palace will be trimmed with silks and treasures from distant lands and faraway ports. And your place in history shall be assured.

**QUEEN
ISABELLA:** (*insistent*) Yes, that all sounds well and fine. But, you have been promising us these things for many years. Why should we trust you now?

**CHRISTOPHER COLUMBUS:** Because the time is ripe. Because Prince Henry of Portugal is funding some of the finest sailors of Europe to search out and establish these sea routes. He knows, as do you, that the Italian cities of Rome and Venice and Naples control the overland routes to the Indies. (*faster*) He knows that those routes are hard and dangerous and that a sea route is the only way to obtain the riches he covets. He knows that time is important. So too, does he wish to have all the glory and all the riches for himself. (*louder and louder*) What then of Spain's place in history? Will Spain be second-rate? Will Spain not prosper from the riches that await in distant lands? (*more passionate*) Will Spain defer to Prince Henry? Will Spain's armada and navy be constrained to the European continent? Does Spain not wish to rule the waves, rule the sea, rule the world?

**KING FERDINAND:** You are, indeed, most fervent in your belief.

**CHRISTOPHER COLUMBUS:** (*somewhat subdued*) I am, your majesty. There is much to discover across the sea—and much to bring back to Spain, her people, and most certainly, her noble rulers.

**QUEEN ISABELLA:** What if we give you the men and ships you seek. Where will you go?

**CHRISTOPHER COLUMBUS:** I will sail west into the setting sun.

**QUEEN ISABELLA:** Is that not dangerous? Are there not monsters awaiting errant sailors?

**CHRISTOPHER COLUMBUS:** I believe not, your highness. I believe that there is but a small ocean to sail across. I believe that the Indies lie just over the horizon.

**KING
FERDINAND:** And how long will this voyage of discovery take you?

**CHRISTOPHER
COLUMBUS:** We shall take but a handful of days. And we shall return with the spices and riches you desire. And, also, we shall return with the glory that is rightfully Spain's and no one else's.

**QUEEN
ISABELLA:** But, we wish much more than just riches and spices. It is the lands you would discover that we also wish. We would give you the authority to claim for Spain any non-Christian lands you might reach. We wish to promote the spread of Christianity throughout the world and the lands you would discover would be converted for the glory of the church.

**KING
FERDINAND:** Our legacy should be a legacy of Christianity and it is through our religion that we rightfully and properly would secure new land.

**QUEEN
ISABELLA:** I believe that your passion has sufficiently swayed me, Christopher. I therefore command you to take charge of our three finest ships and begin your voyage without delay. Go with the knowledge that you are carrying the glory of Spain and the glory of Christianity with you. And, for every land that you discover I shall make you governor. Go wisely, Christopher, and discover what you will.

**CHRISTOPHER
COLUMBUS:** (*head bowed*) I fervently thank you, my queen. You shall not be disappointed. I shall carry the flag of Spain with honor and set it upon the soil of the new land, claiming it once and for all for the greatest country on earth.

**NARRATOR:** Soon after, Christopher Columbus left the court of King Ferdinand and Queen Isabella to begin his preparations for the epic voyage. He and his crew sailed from Spain on August 3, 1492, on the three vessels—the *Nina*, the *Pinta*, and the *Santa Maria*. Two months later, on October 10, 1492, a tiny island (now called Watlings Island), in what is now the Bahamas, was sighted by one of Columbus's men, a sailor named Rodrigo de Triana. Confident that he was in the Indies, Columbus called the people he met Indians.

For several months, Columbus and his crew sailed throughout the islands of Cuba and Hispaniola. The ships eventually returned to Spain—but without the riches and spices Columbus had promised Isabella and Ferdinand. Yet, he thought he would find them on future trips. He made three additional trips to the New World, constantly seeking the elusive route to the West Indies. When he died on May 20, 1506, he believed that he had, in fact, reached the shores of Asia even though he never discovered the riches he had promised.

## Possible Extensions

1. Invite students to rewrite part of the script using one of the following possibilities:

    a. The king and queen refuse Columbus's request.

    b. The king agrees to Columbus's request, the queen does not.

    c. The queen agrees to Columbus's request, the king does not.

2. Ask students to discuss why Columbus Day is celebrated in this country even though Columbus never (in his four voyages to the New World) set foot on what is now the United States.

3. Invite students to create a readers theatre script centering on the events that took place on October 10, 1492.

4. Invite students to investigate early marine maps. Discuss the symbols and creatures depicted on those maps. How are the illustrations on early sea maps different from the ones in use today.

5. Students may enjoy gathering information and data on Columbus's voyages at http://www.mariner.org/age/columbus.html

6. Your students may be interested in reading one or more of the following book selections:

> *Christopher Columbus and the Discovery of the New World* by Carole Gallagher (New York: Chelsea House, 2000).

> *Columbus and the Renaissance Explorers* by Colin Hynson (Hauppage, NY: Barron's, 1998).

> *Follow the Dream* by Peter Sis (New York: Drangonfly, 1996).

> *Where Do You Think You're Going, Christopher Columbus?* by Jean Fritz (New York: Paper Star, 1997).

# An Imaginary Discussion

## Staging

The characters can all be seated on tall stools. There is no narrator; however, a fictitious interviewer (a woman who talks to each of the characters) can be placed at a lectern or podium to the side of the staging area.

|  | John Cabot | Henry Hudson | A Viking |
|---|---|---|---|
|  | X | X | X |

|  | Giovanni da Verrazano | Jacques Cartier |
|---|---|---|
|  | X | X |

Interviewer
X

|  | Samuel de Champlain | Jacques Marquette |
|---|---|---|
|  | X | X |

|  | A Native American | Robert de La Salle |
|---|---|---|
|  | X | X |

[Note: Before performing this script, it is important that students understand that these explorers did not all live at the same time; nor did they necessarily know one another. They all explored different regions of North America at different times.]

**INTERVIEWER:** Let's begin with our Native American visitor. Can you tell us about your life and your claim as the original explorer?

**NATIVE AMERICAN:** Yes. I was originally on this land long before these other explorers (*sweeps his hand*) ever came here. My people have been part of this land for thousands of years. There is no claim by any of these explorers. We have lived on the land and the land is ours.

**INTERVIEWER:** How did you live?

**NATIVE AMERICAN:** We began as big-game hunters. Later, as Ice Age animals died out we turned to food gathering. From there we eventually became farmers. We lived on the land and we took care of the land. We were here for thousands and thousands of years before anyone came across the ocean to explore this land.

**INTERVIEWER:** You may have a point. Right now, I'd like to turn our attention to our Viking explorer. Can you tell us, sir, why you should lay claim to being the original or best explorer of this land?

**VIKING:** Of course. As you know, several of my ancestors, including Eric the Red and Leif Eriksson, sailed from Greenland and landed on these shores. They did this in small ships and without the benefit of ocean maps.

**INTERVIEWER:** So, you feel as though you and your ancestors should be recognized as the first explorers of this land.

**VIKING:** Yes. We endured many hardships. We sailed for these lands many times. We came here long before any of my European friends here. We were the first and probably the best explorers ever to set foot on this continent.

**INTERVIEWER:** You certainly have a strong case. But, let's hear from some of our other visitors, too. Mr. Cabot would you please tell us about your discoveries?

**JOHN CABOT:** Of course. As you know I lived in England during the late 1400s. I wanted to provide England with a trade route to the Indies and so I went to the king of England and asked him to finance a trip. On May 22, 1497, I set sail on my ship, the *Matthew* and headed west for China.

**INTERVIEWER:** What did you discover?

**JOHN CABOT:** Well, after a month of sailing I reached a new land. It wasn't China as I had hoped, but was rather a "newe founde lande." We now call this place Newfoundland, Canada.

**INTERVIEWER:** It seems as though this new land was ripe for all kinds of discoveries. You, Mr. Verrazano, had an interesting voyage, didn't you?

**GIOVANNI DA VERRAZANO:** Yes, I did.

**INTERVIEWER:** Can you tell us more about it?

**GIOVANNI DA VERRAZANO:** Of course. As you know I was originally from Italy, but found that it was more lucrative to sail for France. In 1524 I set out to find the Northwest Passage to the Indies. I was also instructed to locate some sites for French settlements in the new land as well. I knew that there was a large piece of land somewhere between Europe and Asia and thought that the Northwest Passage was the way to get through to it.

**INTERVIEWER:** Did you find the Northwest Passage as you had hoped?

**GIOVANNI DA VERRAZANO:** No, unfortunately, I did not. But I was able to sail along what they now call the coast of North Carolina. I sailed northward and found what is now called New York Bay. I eventually sailed further up the coast discovering many new sites. But, alas, I did not find the Indies or the Northwest Passage.

**INTERVIEWER:** That's unfortunate. But, let's turn our attention now to Mr. Cartier. Can you tell us, sir, about your explorations?

**JACQUES CARTIER:** I'd be glad to. I actually journeyed to the New World as a young boy. My father had taken me along with him when he fished off the coast of Newfoundland in 1507. I liked what I saw and decided to return. Between 1534 and 1543 I made three voyages to North America.

**INTERVIEWER:** What were you looking for?

**JACQUES CARTIER:** Actually, I was looking for two things. Of course, I wanted to discover that Northwest Passage to the Indies. And, as I was ordered by the king of France, I wished to discover great riches of gold. On one of my voyages I sailed down what is now known as the Saint Lawrence River. On the river I came upon a small Indian village. The Indians there helped my men who had come down with a strange disease. My men were cured and we thanked the Indians for all their help.

**INTERVIEWER:** Did you ever find the riches you sought?

**JACQUES CARTIER:** Unfortunately, I did not. But I have heard that our explorations were important in helping to establish the great country of Canada.

**INTERVIEWER:** Thank you, Mr. Cartier. Mr. Champlain, would you mind sharing some of your adventures with us?

**SAMUEL DE CHAMPLAIN:** Why, certainly. I, too, like my fellow explorer Mr. Cartier, knew that the Saint Lawrence River was a great and necessary river in the New World. It was important because it allowed us to trade with the Indians. We could trade furs, guns, and cloth and carry those items up and down the river.

**INTERVIEWER:** So, your main interest was to set up a thriving trade with the Indians in the region?

**SAMUEL
DE CHAMPLAIN:**  Yes. When I explored the river in 1603 and 1604 I wished to establish some fur trading posts. I was able to set up one at the place, now called Montreal, where Mr. Cartier got help from the Indians. I also founded the city of Quebec, which is now the capital of the country of Canada.

**INTERVIEWER:**  So, would you say that you were successful in your ventures?

**SAMUEL
DE CHAMPLAIN:**  I believe so. We showed the importance of trade with the Indians of the New World and we showed how important a mighty river such as the Saint Lawrence was to that trade. I think we were quite successful.

**INTERVIEWER:**  Thanks. I'd now like to turn to Mr. Henry Hudson. Mr. Hudson, would you care to share your explorations with us?

**HENRY HUDSON:**  I'd be happy to. It's important for you to know that I'm originally an Englishman; however, I sailed for the Dutch.

**INTERVIEWER:**  Wasn't that unusual?

**HENRY HUDSON:**  No, actually it wasn't. Explorers sailed for whomever would pay the most money. They didn't necessarily sail for the countries in which they were born.

**INTERVIEWER:**  Hmmm. That's interesting. Can you tell us more?

**HENRY HUDSON:**  Yes. In 1609 I, too, was seeking that elusive trade route to the Indies. I sailed up a great river. I believe that a very large city now lies at the mouth of that river . . . a city you call New York City.

**INTERVIEWER:**  That is correct. Anything else?

**HENRY HUDSON:**  Yes, shortly after sailing up that river I decided to sail for my native country of England. It was in 1610 that I sailed with my men into a great and magnificent bay. That bay is now called Hudson Bay in honor of my discovery.

**INTERVIEWER:** Thank you, Mr. Hudson. Mr. Marquette, could you please tell us about some of the explorations and work you did?

**JACQUES MARQUETTE:** Yes, of course. We knew of the explorations of our French counterparts along the great Saint Lawrence River. But we had also heard of the mighty Mississippi River that was in the country you now call the United States. We knew that there were many Indians and many Indian tribes who lived along that river.

**INTERVIEWER:** And so you went to the Mississippi River in order to set up some trading posts?

**JACQUES MARQUETTE:** No, you see, I was a missionary. My job was to convert all the Indians to Christianity. In order to do that, I traveled with my friend Louis Joliet. Louis was a trader and explorer and he helped us in our travels.

**INTERVIEWER:** Where exactly did you go?

**JACQUES MARQUETTE:** In 1673, we went all the way down the Mississippi River to where it joins with what you now call the Arkansas River. Our journey, as you can imagine, was long and perilous. But we were able to convert many Indians.

**INTERVIEWER:** So, your journey was not to seek riches, but rather to convert Indians?

**JACQUES MARQUETTE:** You are correct.

**INTERVIEWER:** Thank you. Let's now interview Mr. La Salle. Tell us, sir, what was the intent of your explorations?

**ROBERT DE LA SALLE:** I was not an explorer at first, but rather a simple fur trader. I knew, however, that to be successful at fur trading one had to travel great distances. So, I guess, I became an explorer almost by accident.

**INTERVIEWER:** What exactly did you explore?

**ROBERT DE LA SALLE:** I explored a great deal of the Ohio River. But, even more important than that, I also traveled down and explored much of the Mississippi River.

**INTERVIEWER:** When did you do this, sir?

**ROBERT DE LA SALLE:** Much of my explorations took place in the early 1680s. They were important, I guess, because I was able to go all the way down the Mississippi River and into the great Gulf of Mexico.

**INTERVIEWER:** Why was that so important?

**ROBERT DE LA SALLE:** I named all of the land around the mouth of the Mississippi River for our king, Louis XIV. I believe you now refer to that place as Louisiana.

**INTERVIEWER:** I thank you all, gentlemen. It seems as though you have all made important contributions to the discovery of this land we now call the United States. But, now I'd like to turn the discussion over to the members of the audience. Audience, you have now heard from several explorers throughout history. Each has described his life and his explorations. Which of the distinguished explorers who now sit before you would you consider to be the most important in terms of the history of the United States?

[Note: The interviewer can ask individual members of the audience to make a case for one or more explorers. An alternate strategy would be to divide the class into several small groups. Each group is "assigned" an explorer and is asked to plead his case as the most significant or important to the discovery and/or exploration of the North American continent.]

## Possible Extensions

1.  Invite students to select one of the explorers above and to develop a special readers theatre script about that individual.

2.  Encourage students to trace the routes each of the explorers above took throughout the New World. Each route can be traced in a different color on the map. Plan time to discuss the distances traveled by each explorer and some of the challenges he may have faced during a particular voyage.

3.  Invite small groups of students to each select one of the explorers above. Encourage each group to explain why they would want to travel with that individual.

4.  Sir Francis Drake was an English explorer who sailed along what is now the West Coast of the United States. Invite students to research library holdings or Internet resources and to present some of Drake's discoveries between 1577 and 1580. How did his discoveries compare with his French counterparts?

5.  Students may be interested in gathering some information on the Northwest Passage. After appropriate library research, invite them to discuss the significance and importance of the Northwest Passage to England and France during the 1500s and 1600s.

# PART 2

# The Beginnings of a New Nation

## The 1600s and 1700s

# The Mayflower Compact

## Staging

The characters can all be seated on stools or chairs around a large table or desk. The narrator should be standing off to one side of the staging area.

William Brewster
X

John Carver    X        X    Edward Tilley

Issac Allerton    X        X    William Bradford

Myles Standish    X        X    Peter Browne

Narrator
X

**NARRATOR:** The year is 1620. A group of 101 men and women boarded an old ship named the *Mayflower* and set sail for Virginia. Many of these people purchased stock in the Plymouth Company, which hoped to make a profit in the New World.

A small group of individuals on board that ship, later known as the Pilgrims, left England to seek religious freedom in the New World.

As the *Mayflower* heads for Chesapeake Bay, an inlet near Jamestown, Virginia, a fierce December storm drives the ship northward to Plymouth Harbor in what is now Massachusetts. Before setting ashore, William Brewster, the leader of this band of people, wants to make sure that all colonists work together for the good of the colony. He presents an unusual agreement for the men to sign.

**WILLIAM
BREWSTER:**   Good tidings to all who have gathered here. Before we set foot on this new land before us, I wish to present a document to this body. This document has been prepared as a pact—an agreement between all those who gather here and are on board this ship. This pact is for the preservation of our freedoms, for ensuring our liberties, and for guarantees about our religion. Good William, you shall read to us said document.

**WILLIAM
BRADFORD:**   (*standing*) Hear ye, hear ye, hear ye! Following is the compact to which the men gathered here, as well as others, shall agree and sign their names:

"In the name of God, Amen. We whose names are underwritten, the loyal subjects of our respected ruling Lord King James, by the grace of God, of Great Britain, France, and Ireland, king, defender of the faith, etc.

Having agreed for the glory of God and advancement of the Christian faith and honor of our king and country to a voyage to plant the first colony in the northern parts of Virginia, do seriously and together in the presence of God, and one another, combine ourselves together into a political body. We do this for our better ordering and preservation of the ends mentioned before. And for these reasons to enact and plan such just and equal laws, rules, acts, and offices, from time to time, as shall be thought best for the general good of the colony. Unto which we promise all due submission and obedience. In witness thereof we have hereunder signed our names at Cape Cod the 11th of November, in the reign of our ruling Lord King James of England, France, and Ireland the eighteenth, and of Scotland the fifty-fourth. Anno Domini 1620."

**EDWARD
TILLEY:**  I have heard this document, good William and I see that it decrees a form of self-government. By this I suppose that you mean that we shall be set free of the bonds of England, Holland, or any other European country. We shall, as it is in this document, be free to establish our own form of government. Is this not what I read in your pact, dear William?

**WILLIAM
BREWSTER:**  That is correct, Edward. I propose a government that is set by the people. This government shall be one of free will and free rights. We shall be able to set our own laws, laws that are for the basic good of everyone, and laws that shall be written by those assembled here as well as those who follow us in future generations.

**ISSAC
ALLERTON:**  To whom exactly shall be granted the right and privilege to make these laws? Surely you do not suppose that every person in the colony shall be granted the rights and ability to make a law for the colony. To do so would be to invite chaos.

**WILLIAM
BREWSTER:**  According to the provisions of this pact, it is proposed that this right to self-government shall be the right of every person within this colony. But, the right to vote on those laws shall be given only to freemen. By freemen I mean those men who own property in the settlement and who are also good members of the church.

**PETER BROWNE:**  (*insistent*) Why just freemen? Doesn't that leave out others who are also part of this new colony? Doesn't that make our new colony just like the tyranny we left behind? Should not everyone, free or not, have the right and the power to govern?

**MYLES
STANDISH:**  I hear what friend William is saying. (*turning to Peter Browne*) But, my good friend, we cannot assume that all people, all men, have the same education or bearing. The

right to self-govern can only be preserved when learned individuals pass and enforce the necessary laws.

**PETER BROWNE:** (*to Myles Standish*) But, who is to say that only property holders or those who attend weekly church services are the best ones to make the laws? Aren't those who work the land equally qualified?

**MYLES STANDISH:** (*to everyone*) Those who work the land may voice their opinions, but we must be sure that self-governance is maintained and assured by those who are bound to the economics of that land. They stand as the representatives, the voices, of all men—free or otherwise.

**WILLIAM BRADFORD:** This pact then, is a guarantee that this colony shall be self-governed. By self-governance it is meant that the colony is a government of the people, by the people, and for the people. Is that not right, William?

**WILLIAM BREWSTER:** Thou are correct, friend William.

**JOHN CARVER:** But, this government you propose, William, how shall it govern? To have a colony that makes its own laws is both noble and righteous. It is from that understanding between members of the colony that we can exist and prosper. But what is it in this compact that will monitor or oversee the passage and guarantee of those laws?

**WILLIAM BREWSTER:** I shall propose the creation of a General Court. Said court shall be composed of the freemen of the colony and shall be representative of the people of this newfound colony. As a representative body this Court shall set the laws by which we shall be governed. It also shall be the court in which those laws are enforced and ensured. And it shall be the body that shall enact taxes that will provide the moneys we need for our preservation.

**JOHN CARVER:**  How is this court of yours different from those in the old country? It sounds to me like you have created something that is quite similar to that which we left.

**ISSAC ALLERTON:**  Friend John speaks well. I see no difference between this court of yours and the courts of England. English courts were for the rich and were controlled by the rich. They gave no freedoms to the common man. The freedoms were merely illusions. The courts could rule as they wanted. Nothing was ever guaranteed.

**PETER BROWNE:**  Dear William, am I not correct in saying that this General Court is the supreme authority in the colony? I read what you have written and I hear what you are saying and I interpret this body, this General Court, to have great and far-reaching power over this new colony of ours. I do not see how that power is any different than that power under which we lived previously. Please explain it to us.

**WILLIAM BREWSTER:**  I believe that there must be a single governing body that can monitor and debate all that is good for the colony. The decision-making power must reside with that single body to guarantee a balanced government that shall apply equally to each and every person within the colony. Many decisions by many bodies could, perhaps, lead to chaos and the ultimate destruction of the colony.

**ISSAC ALLERTON:**  Would it not be impractical for this General Court to meet with the frequency this document implies?

**WILLIAM BREWSTER:**  You are correct. I propose that the day-to-day affairs of the colony be handled by a governor appointed by the General Court to oversee the enactment and enforcement of the laws of the General Court.

**EDWARD TILLEY:** Are you not proposing, dear William that this governor be a protector of the laws and rules that shall govern this colony? It seems to me that this governor is but a king in a new land. How will this so-called governor be any different from the king we left behind? I fear that there will be little difference, that we will be establishing a ruler with absolute power.

**MYLES STANDISH:** I agree with friend Edward. This governor might take too much power unto himself.

**WILLIAM BRADFORD:** Fear not, dear friends. Such cannot happen. The governor as appointed by the General Court would have his powers monitored by the General Court. Thus, there would be a check and a balance of power within our colony—a system of governance that would ensure our freedoms and our rights and a system of governance that would ensure those rights for a long time.

**WILLIAM BREWSTER:** This document, then, this Mayflower Compact, shall be the first document on self-government in America. When we affix our names to this document we shall be pledging ourselves to a form of government that gives people new freedoms and also ensures that those freedoms shall be guaranteed for all time.

**JOHN CARVER:** Then, let us vote on this Mayflower Compact. Let us decide on the creation of this new government.

**EVERYONE:** Hear, hear!

**NARRATOR:** The Mayflower Compact was presented to the Pilgrims. Forty-one men signed the agreement, which set up a civil government in the new land. This document was to eventually become the standard for a democratic form of government in the new colonies.

In late 1620, the Pilgrims began building a small settlement. They called it Plymouth after the town in England from which they sailed. Nearly half the colonists died during the first winter, but by spring the colony was firmly established. For nearly 70 years this small, independent settlement in New England survived under the rule of self-government.

## Possible Extensions

1.  Invite students to create a "compact" for the classroom. Encourage them to imagine that their class is the first one in a brand-new school. What guarantees, rights, and/or privileges would they want guaranteed in their new "colony."

2.  Obtain and share one of the following books by Kate Waters. Each will provide your students with a unique view of life in and around Plymouth Colony in the early 1600s:

    *On the* Mayflower: *Voyage of the Ship's Apprentice and a Passenger Girl* (New York: Scholastic, 1999).

    *Samuel Eaton's Day: A Day in the Life of a Pilgrim Boy* (New York: Scholastic, 1993).

    *Sarah Morton's Day: A Day in the Life of a Pilgrim Girl* (New York: Scholastic, 1989).

    *Tapenum's Day: A Wampanoag Indian Boy in Pilgrim Times* (New York: Scholastic, 1996).

3.  Here are some other books about Plymouth you may wish to share with your students:

    *Eating the Plates: A Pilgrim Book of Food and Manners* by Lucille Penner (New York: Simon & Schuster, 1991).

    *If You Sailed on the* Mayflower *in 1620* by Ann McGovern (New York: Scholastic, 1993).

    *Pilgrim Voices: Our First Year in the New World* by Connie Roop (New York: Walker, 1998).

    *Who's That Stepping on Plymouth Rock?* by Jean Fritz (New York: Paper Star, 1998).

4.   Students may wish to obtain additional information about Plymouth Colony. The following Web sites can be particularly instructive:

http://www.plimoth.org/Library/pilgrim.htm

http://archnet.uconn.edu/topical/historic/plimoth/plimoth.html

http://pilgrims.net/plymouth

5.   Invite students to discuss what the term "self-government" means to them. How might that concept differ from other forms of government? What are some of its advantages? What are some of its challenges?

6.   Invite students to interview several adults (e.g. parents, community members, elected officials, school board members). What are some of the forms of government that are in place in and around your local community? For example, is the school district under a form of government different from the city or town? Which form of government is most like a "self-government?"

# Mission San Juan Capistrano

## Staging

Each of the characters slowly walks to the front of the staging area and speaks directly to the audience. After each individual presentation, each character walks to the front left portion of the staging area and remains standing while other characters speak their parts. The narrator can be placed at a podium or lectern at the front right portion of the staging area. If possible, simple costuming may be used to differentiate the characters.

                                                    Padre
                                                      X
                                             Soldier
                                                X
                                    Indian Woman
                                          X
                            Indian Man
                                X
                  Junipero Serra
                        X
        Narrator
           X

NARRATOR: In the middle of the 18th century, the Spanish start settlements in what is now California. These settlements are designed to bring religion to the Indians who live in this area. The first of the settlements, or missions as they were called, is built in San Diego in 1769. In November 1776 a Roman Catholic missionary named Junipero Serra (hu-ne'-pero se' ra) founds the seventh of 21 Spanish missions along the California coast. This mission, Mission San Juan Capistrano, is located above the shores of the Pacific Ocean between San Diego and Los Angeles.

JUNIPERO
SERRA: When we arrived to this area we saw great beauty. We saw a beautiful land as far as the eye could see. And we could see a proud and noble people. Now, we want to provide for the spiritual and material needs of these people. We wish to build a sanctuary and a place of refuge for those who live on this beautiful land. And so, with the help of many people—soldiers, missionaries, and native Indians—we build many buildings using the materials of the area. We use mud to make adobe bricks that form the walls of the church, barracks, and work rooms. We create two beautiful fountain areas and many paths lined with native flowers and plants. We build rooms for grinding grain, rooms for making tools, and rooms for processing food. There are kitchens to prepare the food, a small winery, and tanning rooms. Stables for the horses and living quarters for all who work here are built, too. But our grandest achievement is the building of the church at the southeast corner of the mission. It is the only stone church originally built at a mission. This church is the center of our life here; it is where the people come to pray, it is where we hold Mass, and it is the reason for this mission. We are proud of what we build and we hope that it will last for many years so that others might enjoy it and share in its beauty.

NARRATOR: The Indians of this region call themselves the Acagchemem (Ah-ha-SHAY-mem) tribe. After the Spanish arrive, they are renamed the "Juaneno" tribe. We are not sure what these terms mean.

**INDIAN MAN:** Our life was very simple before Junipero Serra and his missionaries came to this land. We lived in small villages that dotted the shore and were sprinkled throughout the hills and valleys. We were a peaceful people, spending our time fishing in the ocean and gathering nuts and seeds. When the Father and his men came, they employed us to help them build the great mission. Now, we work long and hard. And we are taught many new skills. We learn how to tan hides to be used in clothing. We learn how to make wine to be used in the ceremonies of the church. We also build furnaces and are taught how to make many metal items such as knives, keys, and wrought iron. We have a place to live and work and pray. But, our lives are not as simple as they once were. Now, we are told what to do. We are taught a new religion that is unlike our old beliefs. Before the missionaries came we were a free people. Before, we worked for ourselves. Now, we work for someone else.

**NARRATOR:** The missionaries see the Indians as a form of cheap labor as well as an uncultured people who need organized religion to make their lives complete. This labor force comprises both men and women to construct buildings and to provide a means of financial support for the mission.

**INDIAN WOMAN:** We learn how to press the olives to make oil used in cooking. We are taught to make candles, which provide the light for the buildings. And we are instructed in making soap to wash the clothes and ourselves. Many of these items we trade with the great ships that sail along the coast. The money we earn is given to the mission. Our lives have changed with the arrival of the Father and the building of the great mission. Now, we work for someone else, instead of for ourselves. These are different times for us. Our lives are different; our lives are changed. I'm not sure if our lives are better now, but they certainly are changed.

**NARRATOR:** The 21 missions along the California coast are designed to spread religion throughout the region. But, they are also built as forts in order to protect the Spanish interests in North America. Along with the religious leaders who construct and maintain these missions come the soldiers who offer protection and defend the missions from outside attack.

**SOLDIER:** We live in simple quarters in the barracks on the western side of San Juan Capistrano. Our duty is simple. We are to protect the Mission and its people from the Indians who might attack, and help with the work of the Mission. We help to build the great tanning pits and the winery for pressing grapes. Occasionally, our commandant orders us to ride out over the country to scout for Indians or to patrol the open land around the Mission. A soldier's life is hard and there is not much to do during the day. We take care of the horses and livestock, clean and polish our weapons, and repair our clothing. Life is very lonely for a soldier. Boredom is a constant companion.

**NARRATOR:** San Juan Capistrano, like other California missions, has many different people living within its walls. Included are the padres, or priests, who assist in converting the Indians to the Catholic religion and in teaching them new skills.

**PADRE:** To teach and to educate—that is our duty! We are missionaries, spreading religion to all the native peoples and offering them a place of sanctuary. We wish to train the peoples of this land how to survive on their own, how to take from the land while giving back to it. Perhaps, some day they will own this land. We offer them trades and skills that they did not know before. The mission has several shops for making hats, tanning hides, for pressing olive oil, and for carpentry and metal works. These talents, which are important to the lives of the Indians, can be used for the good of all.

We also bring new plants and animals to this region that have not been seen before. We plant and harvest dates, oranges, lemons, apricots, apples, and peaches. We raise different types of animals such as cows, sheep, pigs, and horses. These plants and animals are important to the survival of the Mission and the people who live in and around the Mission.

**NARRATOR:** The primary goal of Father Junipero Serra and Mission San Juan Capistrano is to convert the Native Americans to Christianity. A secondary objective is to teach them skills and trades that will allow them to be self-sufficient. San Juan Capistrano remains as a historical landmark and an important chapter in American history.

# Possible Extensions

1. Each year, on or about March 19, flocks of swallows return to San Juan Capistrano. Invite students to investigate this annual event and some of the celebrations that surround it. Here's a Web site to get them started: http://www.missionsjc.com/mission3.html.

2. Students may wish to collect additional information relative to Mission San Juan Capistrano. Here are some appropriate Web sites:

    http://library.thinkquest.org/3615/mission7.shtml

    http://www.sanjuancapistrano.com/pages/page01.asp?Page=Mission

3. Students may enjoy taking a virtual tour of a California mission. The following Web site offers them an inside look: http://library.thinkquest.org/3615/tour1.html.

4. Divide students into two groups: missionaries and Native Americans. Invite them to debate the function and purpose of the missions. Did they make the lives of the Indians better? Did they accomplish their purpose?

5. Invite students to create their own readers theatre script about life in other California missions. How was it similar to or different from the day-to-day activities of Mission San Juan Capistrano?

# A Conversation with Thomas Jefferson

## Staging

The narrator can be placed at a podium or lectern near the front of the staging area. The three reporters should be standing. Thomas Jefferson can be seated on a stool.

Reporter 1
X

Thomas Jefferson                         Reporter 2
X                                         X

Reporter 3
X

Narrator
X

**NARRATOR:** The time is 1775. The Revolutionary War has begun. The colonists are angry at the laws being imposed on them from England. They feel they are being treated and ruled unfairly. The colonists feel they should be able to pass their own laws. King George of England thinks otherwise.

The Congress decides to tell the king in a public letter that the colonies now consider themselves independent. The job of writing this Declaration of Independence was given to a young lawyer from Virginia, Thomas Jefferson.

As we look in on this fictionalized scene, Mr. Jefferson has just completed drafting the Declaration of Independence, and three newspaper reporters are interviewing him.

**REPORTER 1:**  Mr. Jefferson, I'm Benjamin Bonnely from the *Patriot News*. Can you tell us, please, what you and Benjamin Franklin, Robert Livingston, John Adams, and Roger Sherman hope to accomplish by writing this so-called Declaration of Independence?

**THOMAS JEFFERSON:**  Certainly, Mr. Bonnely. One purpose in writing this document was to tell the world the reasons why the colonists were rebelling.

**REPORTER 2:**  Mr. Jefferson, Patrick Engalls from the *Colonist's Gazette*. Tell me, sir, why exactly are the colonists rebelling against the king of England? Doesn't England provide the colonists with materials and supplies enough to sustain them?

**THOMAS JEFFERSON:**  Well, you see, it's not as easy as all that. You remember back in 1754 when England and France were fighting over the lands in the Ohio River Valley?

**REPORTER 2:**  Yes.

**THOMAS JEFFERSON:**  Well, that war, what you reporters called the French and Indian War, lasted for nearly nine years. It was an expensive war for both sides. The English ran up large debts as a result of the war. The king of England thought that the colonists should help pay for the war and so he levied taxes upon the colonists. Up until that point the colonists had paid taxes to their colonial governments, but now they were being asked to pay taxes to an overseas government.

**REPORTER 3:**  Sir, I'm Cecil Randolph from the *Freedom Press*. Sir, wasn't there another reason why the colonists began to have problems with the English?

**THOMAS JEFFERSON:** Well, yes. After the war, the English wanted the colonists to stay out of Indian lands so that they would not need to protect settlements with their soldiers. But, that did not stop the colonists. They went into Indian lands and began to settle there. Unfortunately, there were many battles between the settlers and the Indians. The settlers called for help from the English, but help never came. Instead, the English passed laws forbidding any settlement west of the Proclamation Line of 1763.

**REPORTER 1:** I suppose that law angered the colonists.

**THOMAS JEFFERSON:** Indeed it did. And there were other laws passed by the British that angered colonists. One was the Stamp Act, which made colonists pay a tax on every letter they wrote and every newspaper they bought.

**REPORTER 2:** I imagine that was not a very popular tax.

**THOMAS JEFFERSON:** Correct. In fact, between 1765 and this year, England imposed many taxes on the colonies and then sent soldiers here to make sure that everyone paid their taxes to the mother country.

**REPORTER 3:** What was done about those taxes, sir?

**THOMAS JEFFERSON:** There were many boycotts. People refused to buy goods, such as cloth, tea, and paper, that were made in England.

**REPORTER 1:** But don't the colonists know that a government needs to raise taxes in order to pay for the services it provides to its citizens?

**THOMAS JEFFERSON:** Yes, that's right. The colonists don't have a problem with the question of taxation; they know that taxes are necessary. The problem was that the taxes were imposed by a foreign government that had no interest in the colonies other than the raising of money. The colonists believed that taxes should be imposed only by elected representatives of the people who had their best interests at heart.

**REPORTER 2:** Isn't that what is meant by "taxation with representation?"

**THOMAS JEFFERSON:** Yes. The colonists didn't want their money going overseas to finance another government. They believed that their money should stay here to be used for the betterment of the colonies.

**REPORTER 3:** Wasn't it shortly after that when the Revolutionary War began?

**THOMAS JEFFERSON:** Yes. Since the battles at Concord, Lexington, and Bunker Hill, the English and Americans have been in a full-scale war. This Revolutionary War is an action by Americans who do not like the way they are being governed. It is also a reaction by the English who claim the authority to govern a colony or group of colonies any way they see fit.

**REPORTER 1:** During the early part of this Revolutionary War you, Benjamin Franklin, Robert Livingston, John Adams, and Roger Sherman met in Philadelphia, didn't you?

**THOMAS JEFFERSON:** Yes, we were there for a meeting of the Second Continental Congress. During that meeting we wrote a letter to King George asking him to repeal the laws that we felt were unjust. As you may recall, he refused to do so.

**REPORTER 2:** So that was what precipitated this Declaration of Independence?

**THOMAS JEFFERSON:** Yes. As Mr. Bonnely stated earlier, we wish to tell the King that we don't like what he is doing and that we want our independence from England. We want to tell him, and the rest of the world, why we are rebelling and about the liberties that we feel we should be granted.

**REPORTER 3:**   So, tell us Mr. Jefferson, what's in the Declaration of Independence?

**THOMAS JEFFERSON:**   There are three main parts to the document. The first part lists all the wrongs that have been done to the colonies by England.

**REPORTER 1:**   What are some of the wrongs you put in the Declaration?

**THOMAS JEFFERSON:**   I stated that England has cut off our trade with the rest of the world. I stated that England has taxed us unfairly and without our approval. And, I wrote that England does not allow us to elect our own representatives.

**REPORTER 2:**   I imagine that you know that those kinds of statements will anger the King.

**THOMAS JEFFERSON:**   Yes, I am well aware of that. But, more important, it is necessary to let the King and the world know that we are being treated and ruled unfairly.

**REPORTER 3:**   What is the second major part of the Declaration of Independence?

**THOMAS JEFFERSON:**   This part may be the most important of all. Basically it says that we do not wish to be ruled by a king. It says that, as a people, we have certain rights that cannot be controlled or governed by any king.

**REPORTER 1:**   What are some of the rights you talked about?

**THOMAS JEFFERSON:**   Here is what I wrote in the Declaration: "We hold these truths to be self-evident: That all men are created equal; that they are endowed by their Creator with certain unalienable rights; that among these are life, liberty, and the pursuit of happiness."

**REPORTER 2:**   Those are very powerful words, Mr. Jefferson.

**THOMAS JEFFERSON:** Yes, they are meant to be. I believe that every human being has rights that cannot be controlled or taken away by any other human being. And people can and should oppose anyone who takes away those rights, even if that person is a king.

**REPORTER 3:** What else did you put in the Declaration of Independence?

**THOMAS JEFFERSON:** The last part of the document is a declaration of war against England. We believe that the time for compromise with England has passed. If England will not grant us our rights, then it is time for us to take our rights.

**REPORTER 1:** This seems to be a most important document . . . a most unusual document.

**THOMAS JEFFERSON:** Indeed it is! It is a document that guarantees certain rights and makes provisions for obtaining those rights.

**REPORTER 2:** What happens now?

**THOMAS JEFFERSON:** The Declaration of Independence will be presented to the Second Continental Congress for a vote.

**NARRATOR:** The Declaration of Independence was presented to Congress on June 28, 1776. However, before it was approved the delegates decided to cut out the part that blamed George III for the slave trade. Delegates from slave states did not want to threaten slave owners who were both rich and powerful. After that, events moved quickly and Congress adopted the Declaration of Independence on July 4, 1776. Since then, the Declaration of Independence has been a model of government for people all over the world. Today, more than 200 years after its signing, it is still a powerful and effective document.

## Possible Extensions

1.  Invite students to imagine that their class is going to rebel against the school. What types of rights or freedoms would they like to include in their "Declaration of Independence?"

2.  Students can access information about the Revolutionary War at the following Web sites. Each site was developed by various classes of elementary and middle school students:

    http://205.161.11.2/student/revwar/revwar.html

    http://www.beavton.k12.or.us/Barnes/revwarreports/revwar.html

    http://tqjunior.advanced.org/3803/photogallery.html

3.  Students can learn more about the Declaration of Independence at the following Web sites:

    http://www.law.indiana.edu/uslawdocs/declaration.html

    http://lcweb.loc.gov/exhibits/declara/declara1.html

    http://www.nara.gov/exhall/charters/declaration/decmain.html

4.  Students may enjoy learning more about Thomas Jefferson. The following books are particularly appropriate:

    *A Picture Book of Thomas Jefferson* by David Adler (New York: Holiday House, 1990).

    *Thomas Jefferson: Man on a Mountain* by Natalie Bober (New York: Aladdin, 1997).

    *Thomas Jefferson: Architect of Democracy* by John Severance (New York: Clarion, 1998).

5.  Invite students to create an original readers theatre script about some of the discussions that may have taken place between Thomas Jefferson, Benjamin Franklin, Roger Sherman, John Adams, and Robert Livingston concerning specific elements to be included in the Declaration of Independence.

# The Delegates Speak Out

## Staging

The characters are all seated on chairs or stools in the middle of the staging area. As each speaks, he stands up and addresses the audience. When done, he sits down and the next character stands and speaks. The narrator is at a podium or lectern at the rear of the staging area.

Narrator
     X

| George Washington | Benjamin Franklin | James Madison | Alexander Hamilton | Roger Sherman | Charles Pinckney |
|---|---|---|---|---|---|
| X | X | X | X | X | X |

**NARRATOR:** In 1787, 55 delegates from 12 of the 13 colonies traveled to Philadelphia, Pennsylvania. There, they created a plan for the governance of this new country—the United States of America. They created the Constitution, a document that gave certain powers to the people of the country. This document ensured that the people would take part in running the government. As a result, the United States would be a democracy.

The delegates had many difficult decisions to make in writing the Constitution. They wanted to make sure it was strong, but not too strong. They also wanted to make sure the Constitution would be able to last for many years. Let's listen to a fictitious conversation by the framers of the Constitution and what they wanted to include in this all-important document.

**GEORGE WASHINGTON:** First of all, I believe that the United States should be a special kind of democracy. A democracy is a government of the people and by the people. But, I think we should go beyond that. This new government should be a republic. A republic is a type of democracy in which citizens govern themselves through elected representatives. The people at special elections would elect all the representatives. Then, they would get together at a central location, the nation's capital, and pass laws to protect and guard the rights of the citizens who elected them. What do you think, Ben?

**BENJAMIN FRANKLIN:** I also want a government that is complete. To do that we should divide the powers of the government into sections, or branches, of government. The first branch should be the Executive Branch. This branch would make sure that the laws of the country would be carried out. This branch of government would include the president and vice-president of the country. What do you think, James?

**JAMES MADISON:** I think we need a branch of government to make the laws. This branch of government should be called the Legislative Branch. In the Legislative Branch there should be two houses, or sections, of government. One section can be called the Senate and the other section can be called the House of Representatives. But we may have a problem with this idea. That is, how many representatives should each state have? The large states will want more representatives than the smaller states. The smaller states will want an equal voice in running the government.

**ALEXANDER HAMILTON:** I think that our friend Mr. Franklin there (*Franklin nods*) has a possible compromise or solution to this problem. When I talked with him, he suggested that each state elect representatives to Congress based on their population. Of course, that meant that larger states would have more representatives in Congress than did smaller states. But, the wise Mr. Franklin also told me something else. It was his idea that each state, regardless of its size or population would elect two senators to Congress. That way, smaller states and larger states would each have the same number of votes in Congress. I believe that both the large states and the small states will like this plan.

**ROGER SHERMAN:** I believe that we also need a third section, or branch for our new country. This branch can be called the Judicial Branch. This branch of government would interpret the laws passed by Congress and decide if any laws had been broken. This branch would consist of all the courts in the country including the Supreme Court.

**CHARLES PINCKNEY:** Well, I think we have a pretty good document—a pretty good Constitution. But, our good friend Mr. Madison there (*Madison nods*) points out something very important. Mr. Madison says that the government would work best if everyone worked together. He also says that no one branch of government should have more power than any other branch. In addition, he points out that it would be best if each branch of the new government could limit the powers of the other branches. He calls this a system of "checks and balances." That means that everybody knows what everybody else is doing. No branch of government has too much power and each branch could watch, or monitor, what the other was doing. I think that Mr. Madison's idea is a good one and that it should be written into the Constitution.

**GEORGE
WASHINGTON:**  We have been working long and hard. We've been discussing, arguing, debating, and compromising for several months and believe that we now have an important document for the new country. But, we still have some work to do. One of the big questions we still have to wrestle with concerns the division of power; that is, how much power should the central government have and how much power should the states have?

**BENJAMIN
FRANKLIN:**  Now, this is getting really interesting. I don't think the central government should be too strong, because that would give it too much power. And, I don't want the states to be too strong because that would mean less power for the central government. So, I'd like to suggest a form of government called federalism. Federalism is a form of government in which power is divided between national, state, and local authorities.

**JAMES
MADISON:**  Let me see if I can understand this federalist idea. First of all, you're saying that the national government is given some very specific powers. These powers are reserved exclusively for the national government. Some of the powers include supporting the armed forces, establishing a postal system, regulating foreign trade, printing money, and declaring war. These powers belong solely to the national government and no one else. Is that correct, Ben?

**BENJAMIN
FRANKLIN:**  Yes.

**ALEXANDER
HAMILTON:**  As I understand it, federalism also ensures that the states each have special powers, too. These powers can only be enforced by each state and the national government cannot tell a state how to conduct its business in these matters. Some of the special powers reserved for the states include conducting elections, licensing businesses, establishing public schools, establishing voting laws, and conducting

elections. In other words, these powers are simply and solely state powers.

**ROGER SHERMAN:** That's right. But here is where it gets really interesting. As you have heard, the national government has a set of special powers and each state has its own set of powers, too. But we also know that if this Constitution is going to be strong, there will also have to be some powers that will be shared by both the national and state governments. This sharing will help ensure cooperation rather than a competition between the states and the national government. Some of these shared powers can include the right to collect taxes, the power to borrow money, and provisions for the health and welfare of the people. These shared powers will help ensure a balanced government.

**CHARLES PINCKNEY:** After we finish writing this new document, we want the Constitution to be ratified, or approved by a majority of the states before it can become law. Some states may like this new document and some states may not. Some may think that it gives too much power to the central government and some may think that it doesn't give enough power.

**NARRATOR:** Between September 17, 1787, and June 21, 1788, nine of the 13 states voted for the new Constitution. That was enough to make the new Constitution the law of the land. This lasting document, which has served as a model for other governments around the world, begins with powerful words. This section, also known as the Preamble, explains the purpose for writing the Constitution. It states: "We the People of the United States, in Order to form a more perfect Union, establish Justice, insure domestic Tranquility, provide for the common defense, promote the general Welfare, and secure the Blessings of Liberty to ourselves and our Posterity, do ordain and establish this Constitution for the United States of America."

# Possible Extensions

1.  Share the Bill of Rights with students. Invite them to discuss reasons why these first ten amendments to the Constitution are so important. Are they just as important today as they were in 1791 when they were first added?

2.  Invite students to create a constitution for their classroom. What form of government should be followed? What are their rights and privileges? How will those rights be protected?

3.  If possible, invite students to attend a school board meeting or town council meeting in your local community. Afterwards, invite them to discuss how powers between several subgroups might be part of a system of "checks and balances."

4.  Other countries have used our Constitution as a model for establishing new governments. Invite students to discuss some of the strengths of our Constitution. Then, encourage them to craft a readers theatre script about the beginnings of a new constitution in another country.

5.  Students may be interested in accessing selected Web sites on the U.S. Constitution. The following are excellent starting places:

    http://www.nara.gov/exhall/charters/constitution/conhist.html

    http://www.law.emory.edu/FEDERAL/usconst.html

    http://rs6.loc.gov/ammem/bdsds/bdexhome.html

# PART 3

# The Nation Changes

## The 19th Century

# With the McMillans on the Oregon Trail

## Staging

The narrator can be placed at a podium or lectern near the front of the staging area. The characters should all be seated on stools or chairs arranged in two rows of three chairs per row (to simulate the positions they might have in a covered wagon). The characters are all facing the direction of the arrow. OPTIONAL: Two students (on their hands and knees) can assume the role of oxen at the front of the covered wagon.

|  | Mr. McMillan | William | Sarah |
|---|---|---|---|
|  | X | X | X |
| ← - - - - - - - - - - - - |  |  |  |
|  | Mrs. McMillan | Peter | Becky |
|  | X | X | X |

Narrator
X

**NARRATOR:**    British fur traders had been in Oregon since the 1700s and had established a profitable fur trade. In 1811, John Jacob Astor built the town of Astoria at the mouth of the Columbia River. Missionaries and traders sent word back to the U.S. describing the beauty and resources of Oregon. These reports attracted many Americans to Oregon.

In 1841, the first wagon train traveled over the Oregon Trail—a trail that began in Independence, Missouri and ended near Portland, Oregon. Soon, other trains were making the 2,000 mile journey across the Great Plains, the Rocky Mountains, and eventually the Willamette Valley.

Let's look in on a fictitious family as they trek across the Oregon Trail in 1842.

**WILLIAM:**    Hey, Pa, how long did you say this trip to Oregon was going to take us?

**MR. McMILLAN:**    According to the wagon master this trip should take us between four to six months.

**BECKY:**    That's a long time, Pa. How come it takes so long to get to Oregon?

**MR. McMILLAN:**    It's a long trail, Becky. There's a big wide prairie that we have to get across.

**PETER:**    Hey, look over there (*he points*). See. There's a big herd of antelope grazing on the side of that mountain. Wow. I've never seen so many animals before.

**BECKY:**    Yes, look at them. There are more animals there than we ever saw back in Illinois. I guess this big wide prairie is just full of all kinds of animals.

**MRS. McMILLAN:**    It sure is a land full of surprises. Remember that herd of buffalo we saw along the Platte River. I can't recall seeing that many animals in one place before. There must have been at least a thousand of them standing around and grazing on the prairie grass.

**PETER:**    (*excited*) Yeah. That sure was a wonderful sight.

| | |
|---|---|
| **MR. McMILLAN:** | I suspect that we're going to see lots of wonderful sights on this journey. |
| **SARAH:** | What else do you suppose we're going to see, Pa? |
| **MR. McMILLAN:** | I suppose that we're going to see those majestic Rocky Mountains everyone's been talking about. |
| **WILLIAM:** | Hey, Pa, are those Rocky Mountains as tall as everyone says they are? I mean, do they really reach up into the sky? |
| **MR. McMILLAN:** | That's what I hear. I also hear that it's going to take a lot of work by everyone in the wagon train to get these wagons across the mountains. The mountains are steep and rocky—it's not the best conditions for wagon travel. |
| **BECKY:** | Do you think we're going to have to climb those mountains by ourselves? I mean can't we just ride in the wagons instead of always walking along beside the wagons? |
| **MRS. McMILLAN:** | I'm afraid not, Becky. I know you don't like walking beside our wagon. I know you don't like the dust being kicked up by the oxen. But that's just the way we have to travel. We can't have too much weight in the wagon or we would never be able to get up and down the hills—much less up and down any mountains. |
| **PETER:** | But why do all the kids have to walk and the adults get to ride in the wagon? |
| **MRS. McMILLAN:** | Because it's better that way. If there's any trouble then your father can take over the driving of the oxen and I can keep track of you kids. It's just the safest way for us to travel. |
| **PETER:** | All right, ma. |
| **MR. McMILLAN:** | Crossing those Rocky Mountains is sure going to be difficult. It will take a lot of time and a lot of work. It's a good thing we've got 32 wagons on this wagon train. We're going to need all the help we can get just to get each wagon up |

and over each one of those mountain peaks in the Rocky Mountains.

**MRS. McMILLAN:**    It seems like this trip is nothing but hard work. But, I think it's going to be worth it. We'll be living in a new place and in a new territory. I truly think all the hard work will be worth it.

**MR. McMILLAN:**    So do I. We knew that this wasn't going to be an easy trip when we signed on. We knew there was going to be some hardships and difficult times. We knew the journey was going to be a long one and wouldn't be easy.

**WILLIAM:**    I'm just worried about winter setting in. I know it's going to be hard getting our wagon across the Rocky Mountains. But it's going to be even more difficult if we don't get across before the winter sets in. We'll never make it if we have to pull or push this wagon through the snows of the Rocky Mountains.

**PETER:**    You know what? I'm a little scared of the Indians. We've never seen Indians before and I'm just afraid of what they might do.

**MRS. McMILLAN:**    Now, don't worry about it. Remember after we saw the buffalo along the Platte River we saw a band of Sioux Indians off in the distance? They didn't do anything. They just sat on their horses and watched us. I think they were more interested in the buffalo than they were in us.

**PETER:**    Maybe you're right, Ma. But I'm still afraid of the Indians.

**SARAH:**    So am I.

**MR. McMILLAN:**    I guess we're all a little afraid of the Indians. But there's lots of us here and we've got lots of rifles and ammunition if we need it. We may see some more Indians along the trail, but the way I figure it—if we don't bother them, then they won't bother us.

**WILLIAM:**    I sure do hope you're right, Pa.

**BECKY:**   After we get across the Rocky Mountains, what happens next?

**MR. McMILLAN:**   Well, according to the wagon master, we come to the promised land of Oregon. We come on down to our new home. We come on down to the place where we'll raise our crops and tend our herds and build our house. We'll come on down to the beautiful Oregon Territory.

**WILLIAM:**   Where do you think we'll live, Pa?

**MR. McMILLAN:**   We don't know yet. Your Ma and I haven't decided that yet. But I do know it will have rich fertile fields and wide open lands and lots of tall trees.

**BECKY:**   Will we live by the ocean, Pa? Can we live by the ocean?

**MR. McMILLAN:**   We'll have to see when we get there. Your Ma and I will take a look around and just see what we see. I don't know yet, but we'll find a place the whole family will like.

**MRS. McMILLAN:**   It will be beautiful, children. We know that. It will be beautiful and we will be able to build our new house and build our new life in Oregon. It sure is exciting.

**MR. McMILLAN:**   Yes, it sure is exciting.

**PETER:**   I can hardly wait.

**NARRATOR:**   The people who crossed the country on the Oregon Trail faced lots of hardships. Indians sometimes attacked, trying to prevent the settlers from moving across their land. There was disease, bad food, snowstorms in the mountains, and lots of dust. Wagons would break frequently and would require repairs. Nevertheless, in spite of all the hardships people continued to cross the country. By 1843 there were more than 5,000 settlers living in the Oregon territory. It was truly an exciting time.

## Possible Extensions

1.  Invite students to make a list of materials and supplies that the early settlers of the Oregon Territory would have needed for their survival. How does that list compare with a list that might have been made by the Pilgrims in the early 1600s?

2.  Invite students to trace the Oregon Trail on a blank map of the United States. What are some of the landmarks, towns, cities, and sites currently located along the remnants of the Oregon Trail?

3.  Encourage students to create a readers theatre sequel to the script above. What adventures would the McMillans have experienced in their new home? What did they discover about the Oregon Territory that they didn't know before their journey?

4.  Students may enjoy learning more about the Oregon Trail through the following Web sites:

    http://www.isu.edu/~trinmich/Oregontrail.html

    http://www.teleport.com/~sflora/ortrail.htm

    http://tqjunior.thinkquest.org/6400

5.  Invite students to plot a journey of 2,000 miles across the continental United States. What supplies would they take with them? What form of transportation would they use? How would their journey be different from a journey on the Oregon Trail in the mid-1800s? How would it be similar?

6.  Your students may be interested in reading one of the following books:

    *A Frontier Fort on the Oregon Trail* by Scott Steedman (New York: Peter Bedrick Books, 1994).

    *The Oregon Trail* by R. Conrad Stein (New York: Children's Press, 1994).

    *The Prairie Schooners* by Glen Rounds (New York: Holiday House, 1994).

# One Day in Gettysburg

## Staging

The narrator can stand at a lectern or podium on either side of the staging area. President Lincoln should be facing either stage left or stage right on the opposite side of the stage from the narrator. He will be reciting the Gettysburg Address throughout this play. The five main characters are part of a gathering of individuals. These individuals represent a larger group of people watching the delivery of the speech, which can be adjusted according to the size of the class.

```
                        X       Jeb       X       X
                                 X
                        Samuel       X       Hanna       X
President Lincoln          X                    X
        X              X       X    John     X      X
                                X          Beth
                    X     X         X       X       X

                                                   Narrator
                                                      X
```

**NARRATOR:** One of the bloodiest and most decisive battles of the Civil War occurred in Gettysburg, a small town in south-central Pennsylvania. Confederate General Robert E. Lee hoped that this battle would help the South gain an important

**71**

stronghold in the North. He believed that a Southern victory would greatly discourage the North and cause President Lincoln to call an end to the war. He also thought it would persuade Great Briton and France to recognize the Confederacy.

On July 1, 1863, Lee's army ran into the Union army commanded by General George Meade. For three horrible days the two armies fought, amassing enormous losses on both sides. On the afternoon of July 3 came the climax of the battle. General George Pickett led 15,000 Confederate soldiers against the might of the Union army. This fight, now referred to as "Pickett's Charge," ended in failure. Finally, on July 4, Lee and his army were forced to retreat. They had suffered nearly 28,000 casualties, while the Union army had more than 23,000 killed or wounded.

Five months later, on November 19, 1863, the cemetery at the Gettysburg battlefield was dedicated as a national memorial. The planners invited President Lincoln, but did not expect him to attend while the war was still being fought. It was at that ceremony that President Abraham Lincoln made a speech to nearly 50,000 people—a speech that was to be known as the *Gettysburg Address*.

**JEB:** Good day to you all.

**ALL:** Good day, Jeb.

**BETH:** Good day, everyone. Is everyone here for the president's speech?

**JOHN:** Yes. I wonder what he's going to talk about?

**SAMUEL:** I don't know. But I do know this: Ever since those first shots were fired at Fort Sumter back in April of 1861, there sure has been a lot of blood spilled.

**HANNA:** And all those boys—those young boys—who lost their lives. My sister's boy was among them; bright kid, not more than 16 years old. He would have made a good farmer, too. But he was given a gun and some ammunition, and, well, I guess you know the rest . . . (*trails off*)

**JEB:**    It's a darn shame. Shot and killed, thousands of them, just shot and killed. Bodies lying all over the fields. That battle at Bull Run in July of 1861 started it all. The Union thought the battle would end the war. They never expected the South to be so strong. That was a tough defeat. I guess people figured that the war was going to be a lot longer than they expected.

**HANNA:**    Hey, let's listen . . . the president's about to speak.

**PRESIDENT LINCOLN:**    (*mightily and powerfully*) "Four score and seven years ago our fathers brought forth, upon this continent, a new nation, conceived in Liberty, and dedicated to the proposition that all men are created equal."

**SAMUEL:**    I'll say one thing, Mr. Lincoln sure does know how to start a speech. It makes me feel good that he helps us remember where we came from, you know, where our country began.

**BETH:**    Yeah, Mr. Jefferson and those men in Philadelphia certainly did get it right back in 1776.

**JEB:**    When you think about all the work they did, it sure does put this war into perspective. I mean, even during a great civil war our country can still exist and can still survive.

**JOHN:**    Shhhh, let's listen.

**PRESIDENT LINCOLN:**    "Now we are engaged in a great civil war, testing whether that nation, or any nation so conceived and so dedicated, can long endure. We are met on a great battlefield of that war. We have come to dedicate a portion of that field, as a final resting place for those who here gave their lives that that nation might live. It is altogether fitting and proper that we should do this."

**BETH:**    Yes sir, Mr. Lincoln sure did hit that nail on the head. Like Jeb said, this country can still survive a great and terrible battle like Gettysburg. It's good to know that all that work in 1776 was not in vain.

**SAMUEL:** Yeah, he sure did. Seems like he wants to make sure that everyone here remembers how important that three-day battle was.

**JOHN:** But even more, he wants us to remember the sacrifices those boys made dying here in Gettysburg. He also wants us to remember all those who died at Antietam, Fredericksburg, and Chancellorsville. I guess what he's saying is that we should never forget all the soldiers . . . that there was a reason why this battle took place.

**HANNA:** It seems a shame that those boys are no longer here. All of them fought hard and well and the blood they spilled was, I suppose, the blood of a country. Maybe in some way, we all died a little bit on this battlefield, as well as other battlefields in the war. But you know, this great country of ours still endures. And we should always remember that.

**PRESIDENT LINCOLN:** "But, in a larger sense, we cannot dedicate—we cannot consecrate—we cannot hallow—this ground. The brave men, living and dead, who struggled here, have consecrated it, far above our poor power to add or detract. The world will little note, nor long remember what we say here, but it can never forget what they did here. It is for us, the living, rather, to be dedicated here to the unfinished work which they who fought here have thus far so nobly advanced."

**JOHN:** I think the president is asking us to continue the fight that the soldiers started.

**BETH:** He makes it seem like we still have some work to do in this country. He makes it seem like all that killing and dying should be worth something.

**SAMUEL:** I guess you're right, Beth. We sure do have a lot more work to do. We don't ever want to forget those poor boys and what they did. And we shouldn't forget what still lies ahead.

**JEB:** What's that?

**HANNA:** We've got to pull this nation back together again. There's been too much fighting and too much dying. There's a big job waiting ahead. And you know what? I think that Mr. Lincoln may be just the man to do it.

**PRESIDENT LINCOLN:** "It is rather for us to be here dedicated to the great task remaining before us—that from these honored dead we take increased devotion to that cause for which they gave the last full measure of devotion—that we here highly resolve that these dead shall not have died in vain—that this nation, under God, shall have a new birth of freedom—and that government of the people, by the people, for the people, shall not perish from the earth." (*The audience cheers and applauds*)

**JOHN:** Well, that was one heck of a speech. He sure did say a lot in just a few words.

**JEB:** And he sure did make us think about why we're here, why we came to this place today, and, I guess, why we should continue to come together.

**BETH:** Those young boys and what they died for was sure important. I suppose that this event today might be something for us all to think about. Those boys DID fight for something. I guess in a way they fought for all of us.

**JOHN:** Yeah, they fought for the whole country. Remember what Mr. Lincoln said about "these dead shall not have died in vain"? I think he was telling us all something very important.

**HANNA:** Yes, it was something we should never forget. And our children's children should never forget either.

**NARRATOR:** The Battle of Gettysburg was not the end of the war. It did, however, signal the overwhelming power of the Union army. Other battles and more fighting took place throughout the next several months. The Union army marched through the South wreaking havoc on cities, towns, railroads, and bridges. In the fall of 1864, President Lincoln was reelected to another term of office. Less than a year later, on April 9, 1865, the South surrendered. Five days after that, on April 14, 1865, President Lincoln was assassinated by John Wilkes Booth.

The Civil War was an important milestone in American history. It settled the argument of federal authority over state's rights. But, in a larger sense, it was a war that touched every part of the country and almost every American. Nearly 600,000 soldiers died during the Civil War—the most of any war the U.S. has fought. Lincoln's brief address on a battlefield in Pennsylvania was one of the most memorable, and certainly one of the shortest events of the conflict.

## Possible Extensions

1. Invite small groups of students to rewrite the Gettysburg Address in their own words. Plan appropriate time to discuss the various interpretations.

2. Encourage students to discuss the feelings that may have been going through the audience listening to this famous speech. How would members of the audience who lost loved ones in the Battle of Gettysburg have felt listening to the president's speech?

3. Students can obtain detailed information about the battle at Gettysburg (appropriate for recording on a timeline) at the following Web site:

   http://www.on-the-square.com/benscivilwar/battlefields/
   gettysburg.htm.

4. Students can see drafts of the Gettysburg Address, techniques used in preserving the original drafts, and the only known photograph taken of President Lincoln at Gettysburg at http://lcweb.loc.gov/exhibits/gadd/ga.html.

5. Students can learn all about Abraham Lincoln including significant events in his life at http://www.historyplace.com/lincoln.

6. Your students may wish to read one of the following books about Gettysburg and the Gettysburg Address:

   *Charley Waters Goes to Gettysburg* by Susan Sinnott (Brookfield, CT: Millbrook Press, 2000).

*Gettysburg* (Battlefields Across America) by Christopher Hughes (Brookfield, CT: Millbrook Press, 1998).

*The Gettysburg Address* by Abraham Lincoln (Boston: Houghton Mifflin, 1995).

*The Gettysburg Address* (Cornerstones of Freedom) by Kenneth Richards (New York: Children's Press, 1992).

*Just a Few Words, Mr. Lincoln: The Story of the Gettysburg Address* by Jean Fritz (New York: Price, Stern, Sloan, 1993).

# Driving the Final Spike

## Staging

The narrator can sit on a stool or stand at a lectern on the side of the staging area. The characters should all be standing in a loose-knit group. They can occasionally move around as they are speaking to each other.

```
        Placer
         X          Sally
                      X          Frenchy
        William                    X
           X         Barbara
                        X          Lily
                                    X

                                              Narrator
                                                 X
```

**NARRATOR:** The year was 1862. The great American West was opening up as pioneers—rich and poor, young and old, white and black—moved from the crowded cities of the East and into the wide-open spaces of the Great Plains. Pioneers from throughout Europe came as well. This was a promised land—a land of extremes, but also a land of enormous possibilities.

The United States government was giving this land away. The Homestead Act of 1862 said that anyone could claim 160 acres of land for free if the homesteader lived on the land and raised one crop within five years. The settlement of this land was hastened by the building of a railroad line from coast to coast. Two companies formed, the Central Pacific Railroad and the Union Pacific Railroad, to build this railroad line. The Central Pacific started building from Sacramento, California heading east through the high Sierra Nevadas. The Union Pacific Railroad began its line in Omaha, Nebraska and headed west across the Great Plains.

After seven years, the two railroad lines met at Promontory Point, Utah on May 10, 1869. A golden spike was hammered in to hold the last rail in place. The first transcontinental railroad was completed.

[Note: If available, you may wish to show students the famous photograph taken on May 10, 1869, of the celebration in Promontory Point, Utah. This photo has been reproduced in many textbooks.]

**PLACER:** Well, my friends, that sure is a pretty sight. Those two locomotives standing there—one from the east, one from the west.

**SALLY:** What do you mean? The way I see it, it's nothing but trouble. Look at those two locomotives belching smoke and making all that noise. Why, they're scaring the horses and frightening all the livestock. Every time one of those locomotives comes through a town every animal for miles around is going to get scared.

**WILLIAM:** I'm not so sure, Sally. Sure, there are going to be lots of changes in the next few years. This probably means that there will be lots of new settlers coming to the West. All those trains crossing the country now will be bringing lots more folks. I figure the more folks we have in the West, the better our chances are for gaining statehood.

**FRENCHY:**   It sure does seem a shame, though. Why, I can recall when I was young that this was nothing but wide-open spaces; people could travel all day by horseback and never see another living soul. A man could build a home for the family and not have a neighbor for miles and miles. Sure do remember those days. Guess it just won't be the same anymore.

**BARBARA:**   Aw, why don't you just quit your moaning and groaning? Seems like all you ever do is complain. See, the way I figure, these trains are going to bring us prosperity. You know, they're going to bring some goods and products and other things from those factories in the East. They're going to bring things we've never seen before. Fine things. Good things. That has to be good for the local economy. It's going to help out all the merchants in town; it's going to help out the whole town.

**LILY:**   Hey, look. I'm all for progress, but my husband and I just don't like these trains and all. Laying those railroad tracks across the frontier takes up good land that could be used by farmers and ranchers or for building houses and towns. All they're doing is crisscrossing the land with their shiny rails and cutting it up so that it can't be used by folks who are trying to make a decent living. The way we figure it, these railroad companies are just taking over the land that rightfully belongs to the people.

**PLACER:**   Lily, I don't understand what you're griping about. Why, you and your husband John got a nice place outside of town. You've got a nice herd of cattle and a small place to do some farming. You should be happy. This railroad can only be good for the country.

**LILY:**   I don't know. It used to be quiet around here. I remember when our family moved here about 10 years ago that it was nice and quiet. I just don't like this "iron horse" eating up all the land and making all that noise.

**FRENCHY:**   It sure isn't like the old days. But, I guess it was bound to happen. Too many people pouring into this country. I hear that those cities in the East are just overflowing with so many people, they just don't know what to do with them. I guess the only place they can send them is out our way. It sure isn't going to be the same, though.

WILLIAM: Yeah, you got that right! Seems like there's been a lot of people from those European countries, too. Seems like a lot of them are coming here to seek their fortunes and their freedoms. They sure must have it hard over there in Europe. It sure must be tough there with those dictators and kings and princes and stuff. Must be hard for people to live like that.

BARBARA: Yeah, just look at all the people around here today. Over there you see those Chinese folk who helped to build the Central Pacific line in here from Sacramento. Heck, I'll say one thing, they sure were good workers on the railroad line. They put in long days and long hours keeping the line open. Hard workers, that's what they were, hard workers. Why, I'd be proud to have them in this country of ours. We need people who aren't afraid of hard work to make this country strong.

PLACER: I'm not so sure. I mean, America is supposed to be a land of opportunity, but I'm not sure we should have lots of those foreigners over here. It seems like more and more of them are coming here taking up land that belongs to us, living in cities that we built, and speaking their strange languages that we can't understand. I'm just not convinced that we need a lot of foreign people here to settle the land. I mean, we've done all right before. Why do we need the railroad to bring in more people from overseas?

SALLY: I think you've got it all wrong, Placer. Those two railroads went through all kinds of territories and the people who built them went through all kinds of trouble just to get them tied up from coast to coast. And now we've got the entire country hitched up like two pigs in a trough. That just makes us a stronger country. Now, we can send people and products from coast to coast as fast as ever. I mean, these two railroads have done something that's never been done before.

**LILY:** I just don't think I can agree with you. It sure seems like a lot of noise and a lot of valuable land has been wasted just so we can have people from the east or from Europe come into these wide open spaces of ours. I just don't like it. I don't like it at all!

**WILLIAM:** But, Lily, the more people we have here the more people we have to make this land productive and strong.

**FRENCHY:** Yeah, I suppose there's going to be lots of changes in store. Sure do wish I could see into the future so I could see what this will all mean 20 or 50 years from now.

**SALLY:** Yeah, there's a lot about to happen. This Golden Spike could be just the beginning of some good things for the whole country.

**BARBARA:** It sure is exciting.

**LILY:** I just don't know. I'm scared of what it might bring. I'm scared at what we're looking at. I'm scared of the future for this land of ours. I see trouble and I see problems and I'm scared!

**NARRATOR:** The sound of the Golden Spike being hammered into the Utah soil was said to echo across the Great American Frontier. It signaled the end of one era and the beginning of a new one. It reverberated from shore to shore, and summoned people from across the ocean to this land. It was a trumpet call to those who lived here that the West was ready for the people and goods that would crisscross it and change it forever. And it was a signal to the men and women of this land that the country was growing in new directions and new dimensions.

# Possible Extensions

1.  Invite students to discuss any comparisons between the linking of the country via the transcontinental railroad in the 1860s, the linking of the states with interstate highways in the 1950s and 1960s, and the linking of the country via the Internet today.

2.  Students can learn about the transcontinental railroad via the following Web sites:

    http://www.mindspring.com/~jjlanham/trcc1.htm

    http://www.blm.gov/education/railroads/trans.html

3.  Students can learn about the laying of the Golden Spike at Promontory Point, Utah by accessing the following Web sites:

    http://www.sfmuseum.org/hist1/rail.html

    http://www.NPS.GOV/GOSP

4.  Invite students to create their own readers theatre script about several Europeans witnessing the driving of the Golden Spike on May 10, 1869. How would their interpretation differ from that presented in the script above?

5.  Invite students to create a map of the different railroad lines that crisscrossed the country in the years following the laying of the transcontinental railroad. What did all these railroad lines mean for the economy and settlement of the West?

6.  Your students may enjoy the following children's books about the building of the transcontinental railroad:

    *Full Steam Ahead: The Race to Build a Transcontinental Railroad* by Rhoda Blumberg (Washington, DC: National Geographic Society, 1996).

    *Ten Mile Day: And the Building of the Transcontinental Railroad* by Mary Ann Fraser (New York: Henry Holt, 1996).

    *The Transcontinental Railroad* by Thomas Streissguth (San Diego, CA: Lucent Books, 1999).

# The Shapiros' New Adventure

## Staging

The narrator can sit on a stool or stand at the rear of the staging area. The four main characters can be standing or may be seated on stools. If possible, hang an old sheet in the background with waves painted on it to make it seem as though all the action is taking place on a large ship.

Narrator
X

Papa
X

Mama
X

Miriam
X

Ben
X

**NARRATOR:** The year is 1892. Thousands of people in eastern and southern Europe are flocking to the shores of America to seek new land, religious freedom, and political independence.

Most of these immigrants are from southern and eastern Europe, primarily from Italy, Poland, Russia, and Hungary. People in these regions of the world are facing economic disaster. Unemployment, overpopulated cities, and unproductive agricultural techniques are spurring many people to travel to "The Land of Plenty"—the United States. Many people suffer religious persecution as well. Jews, for example, are forbidden to own land, engage in certain trades, or move out of areas that have been set aside for them. As a result, there is widespread poverty and discrimination. Many immigrants see the United States as a place of personal safety, religious freedom, and economic opportunity.

One such family is the Shapiros (a fictitious family). The Shapiros are from Russia, and because they are Jewish they have suffered a great deal of persecution. Their beliefs have not been tolerated and they find their life more and more difficult each day. They have heard of a new land, America, where there is plenty of space and plenty of freedom. It is a land of both promise and opportunity. After many weeks of thinking, the Shapiros decide to set sail for this new land—leaving behind everything they have known.

As we look in on the Shapiros, they are on a large steamship bound for America. They are hopeful, yet still worried.

**MIRIAM:** Papa, tell me again about this new land. What is it like?

**PAPA:** It is a land of opportunity, daughter. It is a land where people can find work, where they can find good housing, and where families can be together.

**MIRIAM:** But, I am frightened, father. I am leaving all my friends behind. We are leaving behind our village and our home for a place we know little about.

**MAMA:** Rest easy, child. We are all frightened. We are all a little unsure of what lies before us. Just look around. Over there (she points) are the Krinsky's. An old grandmother and seven children in the family and they, too, have decided to sail to America. Do you not think they are as frightened as we are?

**BEN:** (*pointing*) And look over there. The Paduks have left a profitable dressmaking business to go live in America. We are all leaving that with which we are familiar. We are all travelers on an unknown sea, not knowing what we will find or where we will live.

**PAPA:** You are right, son. We all—every one of us on this ship—seek a better life. Yes, we do not know what that life holds for us. But, we do know that it must be a life much better than the one we leave. There must be a carpenter's job for me so I may put bread upon our table. There must be a seamstress's job for your mother to help us pay the rent. And there must be good schools for both of you (points to the two children) to learn English and to do math.

**MIRIAM:** Oh, Papa, you are always thinking the best. But, I am still scared. We do not know the people in this new land; we do not know their ways; we do not know their language. What will they think of us? What will they say about us?

**MAMA:** Your papa and I are scared, too, my child. It is a big adventure for everyone. There are many things we do not know. There are many things we will need to learn. There are many things that await us.

**NARRATOR:** The trip from Europe to the United States is not easy. Besides the cost of the trip, the hardships of travel make the journey even more difficult. Many immigrants have to book passage in steerage, a section of the ship set aside for people who pay the lowest fares. Generally, the accommodations are crowded, dirty, and uncomfortable.

The Shapiros are about halfway through the trip. The conditions on board are barely tolerable. Word filters through the immigrants that there have been some deaths due to the crowded and unsanitary conditions.

**BEN:** Papa, I have just heard about another family in steerage. The word is that two of their children have died from high fever.

**PAPA:** I have heard that, too. It is very crowded in here and I am sure that it is not as sanitary as we would like it to be.

**MAMA:** I'm afraid that there might be others who will not be able to see the new land. There will be other deaths and other burials at sea. This is not an easy journey for anyone.

**BEN:** Why do so many have to die? Why is this journey so long and so dangerous? I do not like the bad food we have to eat or the dirty beds we have to sleep in. I am afraid that one or more of us will get very sick. This is not what I thought the journey would be like.

**MIRIAM:** I, too, am frightened. I do not like this ship or the people who run it. I do not trust them and they seem not to notice the passengers. We are like baggage to them.

**MAMA:** Do not worry so, child. In a short time we shall be docking in our new country—our new land—and then everything will be all right. Just be patient, my child. Just be patient.

**NARRATOR:** Upon their arrival in the United States all immigrants had to be checked for any criminal records or communicable diseases. This processing took place at Ellis Island in New York Harbor. Ellis Island is next to the Statue of Liberty, which was a symbol of hope for a better life for many immigrants.

It is now nearing the end of the voyage and the Shapiros, like most of the immigrants on board the ship are eager to see their new land. Excitement is high and conversation is lively as the ship nears New York Harbor.

**MAMA:** Your Uncle Levi wrote to us of New York City and told us that we would sail into the harbor and pass by the great statue of the famous lady.

**MIRIAM:** Famous lady?

**MAMA:** Yes, they her call Lady Liberty. I believe that Uncle Levi called her the Statue of Liberty. (*reflective*) Liberty . . . ah, what a sweet word!

**MIRIAM:**    Then what, Mama, then what?

**MAMA:**    Then we will get off the ship at a place called Ellis Island where all people new to America arrive. There will be many of us there: adventurers, travelers, and explorers from all over the world.

**PAPA:**    We will be with many freedom-loving people from the world over who, like us, seek a new life.

**BEN:**    I have heard that we will be given new names . . . American names . . . a new family name.

**PAPA:**    Perhaps. But, we will become Americans. And most important, we will become free. We will be free of the tyrants of our old land. We will be free of the persecution we faced every day. We will be free of the poor land of our ancestors. We will be Americans . . . free Americans!

**MIRIAM:**    I am still anxious, Papa.

**PAPA:**    So am I, dear Miriam. And so is your Mama. And so is your brother.

**MAMA:**    Yes, my child, we are all anxious but we are also filled with hope. And that hope and our faith will help us make good in our new land.

**PAPA:**    We will survive and we will succeed. It will not be easy; there may be difficult times ahead, but we will live a better life.

**MIRIAM:**    I hope you are right, Papa, I hope you are right.

**BEN:**    So do I, so do I.

**NARRATOR:**    A few days later, on a misty, chilly morning, the ship sails into New York Harbor. They pass by the Statue of Liberty—their first view of their new country. A short time later the ship docks at Ellis Island. There, along with 1,200 other passengers, the Shapiros set foot on a new homeland. There are no promises here—only possibilities. For all of the adventurers, there are lots of questions and unknowns, but there is also lots of hope. It is with that hope that the Shapiros begin the first day of their new life in a new country.

Most immigrants, like the Shapiros, have to adjust to life in their new land. Most settle in the cities because that's where most of the jobs are. Others settle on farms and take up a lifestyle that they were accustomed to in their old country. Many immigrants settle in communities made up of people from the same area of origin. This provides them with opportunities to practice familiar celebrations and customs. It is a new land, but one filled with old traditions.

## Possible Extensions

1. Invite students to talk with their parents, grandparents, or other relatives about their ancestral roots. What countries did their families emigrate from? Why did the family emigrate to the United States? Provide opportunities for students to discuss their families' experiences with the whole class.

2. Invite students to investigate the history of Ellis Island. Small groups of students may wish to log on to one or more of the following Web sites in order to collect information that could be displayed on a bulletin board or in an informational brochure or flyer:

   http://www.historychannel.com/ellisisland/

   http://www.ellisisland.org

   http://cmp1.ucr.edu/exhibitions/immigration_id.html

   http://www.neco.org

3. Invite students to create a series of maps that plot the countries (and the number of people from each country) from which people emigrated during the late 1800s and early 1900s.

4. Invite students to discuss some of the conditions possibly experienced by people in other countries that may have prompted them to emigrate to America. Discuss some of the fears that immigrants must have had in making the decision to emigrate. Invite students to consider what would make them leave their country and travel to a new and relatively unknown country far away.

5.   Invite small groups of students to each create a readers theatre script about the first few weeks the Shapiros spent in New York City. Where do they live? What jobs do they get? What do they learn in school?

# Long Hours, Long Days

## Staging

The characters can all be seated on stools or chairs in the center of the staging area. Each worker can be simulating the movement of his/her work (for example, the man can be moving sheets of paper [leather strips] from one pile to another; the woman can pretend to be working a sewing machine, etc.). The narrator/interviewer is at a lectern or podium at the side of the staging area.

|  Man | Woman | Child 1 | Child 2 |
| --- | --- | --- | --- |
| X | X | X | X |

Narrator/Interviewer
    X

**NARRATOR:** During the late 1800s, many machines were invented. These new machines helped change the face of American industry. Machines such as the typewriter, the telephone, the electric light bulb, the cash register, the fountain pen, the adding machine, and the vacuum cleaner made life easier and production more efficient. Other machines helped people do their jobs faster. More goods could be produced in less time.

**91**

The new inventions helped businesses grow and stimulated the growth of brand new industries. More factories were built and more people were needed to operate the machines in those factories. There seemed to be plenty of work for everyone. But all was not as rosy as it seemed. Let's ask our workers here some questions.

**INTERVIEWER:** Tell us, sir, where do you work?

**MAN:** (*slowly and sadly*) I work in a very large and very dark shoe factory along with 2,000 other people. I operate a machine that sews the upper part of a shoe to the sole of the shoe. The machine can do this work very quickly. All I do is put the leather into the machine and the machine sews the parts together. Then, I take that part of the shoe out of the machine, put it in a box, and put another piece of leather into the machine.

**INTERVIEWER:** How long do you work each day?

**MAN:** I do my work over and over and over again. Just put a piece of leather in the machine and take a sewn piece of leather out of the machine. One piece goes in and one piece comes out every 90 seconds. Every hour I put in 40 pieces of leather. Every hour I take out 40 pieces of leather. I do that for 15 hours every day. That's 600 pieces of leather to put into the machine every day. That's 600 pieces of leather to take out of the machine every day. Every day, 600 pieces of leather for 600 shoes.

**INTERVIEWER:** How many days a week do you work?

**MAN:** I work for six days every week from Monday through Saturday. Six days a week, 15 hours every day. That's 90 hours every week. Ninety hours a week putting pieces of leather into a machine and taking pieces of leather out of a machine. Hour after hour; day after day; week after week. Always doing the same thing. That's all I do. That's my job—feeding a machine pieces of leather. All the time feeding a machine pieces of leather. Over and over and over and over. That's my job.

**NARRATOR:** The "sameness" of factory work was everywhere. Both men and women worked in factories, often doing repetitive jobs for very low wages. But in many cities, factory jobs were the only jobs available, particularly for unskilled workers.

**INTERVIEWER:** Excuse me, ma'am. Could you please tell us about your work?

**WOMAN:** (*dejectedly*) I work in a shirt factory with many other people. There are many of us in that factory, working together sewing shirts. We get pieces of cloth and put them into sewing machines. We sew the pieces of cloth together for part of a shirt. All day long we sew shirts. We do nothing else but sew shirts. That's what I do. I sew shirts. And so do the other 450 people in this factory. I sew collars on shirts. Every day I come to work I know what my job is going to be. I know I will sew collars on shirts. Every day I sew collars. It takes me two minutes to sew a collar on a shirt. I can sew 30 collars on 30 shirts in an hour. That's a collar every two minutes.

**INTERVIEWER:** How many other people work in the same room as you?

**WOMAN:** There are 75 of us in this very crowded room. All of us sewing collars on shirts. There is not much room to move around. We must stay in our chairs at our sewing machines. We work through the morning. At 12:00 the whistle blows. Then we can go down to the bathroom. Then we can go to the lunchroom. We open our lunch bundles and eat our lunch in 10 minutes. Then we can talk or sing for 20 minutes. In 30 minutes it is all over. We must go back to our sewing machines. We must go back to sewing collars on shirts. We must go back to sewing 30 collars on 30 shirts every hour.

**INTERVIEWER:** That sounds like very exhausting work. You must be very tired doing that kind of work all the time.

**WOMAN:** We are tired. We are hurting. We are sore. But this is all we can do. We can only sew collars on shirts. Day after day, this is what we do. I work for 74 hours every week sewing collars on shirts. For that 74 hours I am paid $14. I am paid $14 for my entire week of sewing collars on shirts.

**INTERVIEWER:** Why don't the workers get together to force the management to improve the working conditions?

**WOMAN:** That would never work.

**INTERVIEWER:** Why not?

**WOMAN:** Because workers are so cheap to find. Everybody needs a job to feed his or her family and there are more workers than there are jobs. So, if a group of workers decided to ask for better working conditions, the bosses would just fire them and hire some new people.

**INTERVIEWER:** But that doesn't seem fair.

**WOMAN:** It's not fair, but it's all we have.

**INTERVIEWER:** Do you mean to tell me that if you asked for better conditions, you'd be out of a job?

**WOMAN:** That's right. And even more important, I probably wouldn't be able to find another job in this town. I'd have a black mark next to my name and nobody would ever want to hire me.

**INTERVIEWER:** So you're stuck doing a job that you don't like and that has lousy working conditions?

**WOMAN:** That's right. We have to put up and shut up. There's no other way.

**NARRATOR:** Not only were men and women subjected to the repetitive work of factory life; so, too, were children. In fact, more than one-third of the entire work force in the late 1800s comprised children. Children were hired by factories simply because they could be paid less for doing the same amount of work as an adult.

**INTERVIEWER:** Excuse me, can you tell me what you're doing here?

**CHILD 1:**  (*bored*) I'm working in a cotton mill. I'm putting spools of thread on a large machine. I'm putting spools of thread on a large machine and then threading the machine. I'm working on big machines. I'm working on big machines that use spools of thread. I'm working on big machines that have many spools of thread and many places to thread the spools. All day long I put spools of thread in large machines. I don't know how many spools of thread I put on the machines. The machines are running all the time and they use a lot of thread. The machines work fast and so I must work fast. I must watch the entire machine because the machine has many many spools of thread on it. The machine goes around and around and turns the thread into large pieces of cloth.

**INTERVIEWER:**  That sounds like hard work. Don't you ever get a break?

**CHILD 1:**  Much thread is needed for the large pieces of cloth. The machines go all the time. And all the time I must put new spools of thread on the machine. All the time I must thread the machine with the new spools. Over and over and over again I do the same thing.

**INTERVIEWER:**  What about your working conditions in the factory? Can you tell us what kind of conditions you must endure?

**CHILD 1:**  It is hot in the factory. It is *very* hot in the factory. I get hot when I work. I get *very* hot when I work. There are no windows to open in this large factory. We work in a very large room with no windows and lots of machines. I work for 10 hours all day long. Ten hours putting spools on thread on the machine. For 10 hours of work I am paid 10¢. I am paid one cent for each hour I work.

**INTERVIEWER:**  That doesn't sound like very much. Why don't you get another job?

**CHILD 1:**  Jobs are cheap. Children are cheap. All the jobs for children pay very little. That's all there is.

**INTERVIEWER:**  Why are you working in the first place? Why aren't you home with your family? Why aren't you in school?

**CHILD 1:**   My whole family works. We all need to work in order to survive. If everyone didn't work we wouldn't have a place to live and we wouldn't have food to eat. I don't go to school because if I went to school then we would lose all the money that I bring in. And then we might be thrown into the street.

**INTERVIEWER:**   It sounds like a tough life.

**CHILD 1:**   Yeah. It's a tough life.

**NARRATOR:**   Children worked long and hard in many factories and industries. Many families needed the money earned by children in order to survive. Thus, when children reached a certain age, perhaps as young as seven, they were sent off to work and earn money for the family. Their lives were hard and so were the working conditions.

**INTERVIEWER:**   Can you tell us about what you do?

**CHILD 2:**   (*sadly*) I work in a mine. Every day I work in a mine. I come to the mine at 6:00 in the morning. I don't leave the mine until 6:00 at night. I work inside the mine for 12 hours every day. Every day I go into the mine and push out a coal car filled with coal. Two of us are assigned to a coal car and we must push it out of the mine to the top. I am nine years old and I am strong and I spend all day long pushing coal cars to the top of the mine. The work is hard and the work is long. All day I am in the darkness of the mine pushing coal cars.

**INTERVIEWER:**   That sounds like dangerous work.

**CHILD 2:**   Yes, the work is dangerous. My friend Billy had the fingers of his hand crushed by a coal car. There was no doctor. The other miners put a bandage around his hand and told him to work some more. His hand hurt, but he had to work. That was two weeks ago. All the bones were crushed in his hand and now his hand does not work anymore. But he still works in the mine. He still must work in the mine. He was a lucky one.

**INTERVIEWER:**  What do you mean he was the lucky one?

**CHILD 2:**  Dolly used to work putting coal into the coal cars. She would pick up coal from the floor of the mine and put it into the coal cars. All day long that's what she did. One day she wasn't paying attention. A coal car was still moving along the track. Dolly wasn't looking. She had her foot on the track. The coal car ran over her foot. They put a bandage over her foot, but it was too late. Dolly lost some toes on her left foot. Dolly doesn't work here any more. She can't walk right. She can't work in the mines.

**INTERVIEWER:**  What happened to her?

**CHILD 2:**  I heard that she is now working in a factory in another town. I think the factory is a sewing factory. I think they make shirts. Dolly can sit down and make shirts all day long. Maybe she is lucky after all. She can just sit down and make shirts all day long.

**NARRATOR:**  The Industrial Revolution was a time of change . . . a time of change for individuals and a time of change for the country. It meant the mechanization of American society. It meant more machines doing more work. It also meant more jobs. People were needed to run the machines and labor was cheap. The owners of many factories knew that for every worker hired, there were more to replace that individual if he or she didn't work out. There was talk of forming labor unions to fight for the rights of workers, but in the early days of the Industrial Revolution it was just talk. The factory owners had all the power; there was little that the workers could do. Nevertheless, these events set the stage for the eventual rise of labor unions, organizations that fought for the rights of workers. In many ways, these labor unions were an inevitable outgrowth of the entire Industrial Revolution. It could be safely said, that for better or worse, the Industrial Revolution would have a major impact on American society for years to come.

## Possible Extensions ━━━━━━━━━━━━

1.  Invite students to consult Web sites and library resources to obtain information on child labor laws, particularly those passed in the early 1900s. Plan time for students to share their findings.

2.  Invite students to collect information on wages paid to young workers (fast-food servers, newspaper carriers, etc.). How do those wages compare with the wages paid to children in the late 1800s?

3.  If possible, invite a factory worker or the owner of a local factory to discuss working conditions today in comparison with the working conditions of factories in the late 1800s. How have those conditions changed?

4.  Students may be interested in gathering some additional information about the Industrial Revolution via the Internet. Check out the following:

    http://tqjunior.advanced.org/4132

    http://members.tripod.com/xu_chen/indusrevolt

    http://members.aol.com/mhirotsu/kevin/trip2.html

    http://hammer.ne.mediaone.net/lowell/lowell.html

5.  Invite students to discuss any repetitive jobs or chores that they do. How long could they do those jobs over and over again during the course of one day? One week? What makes repetitive work so boring?

6.  Your students may wish to consult one of the following books for additional information on the Industrial Revolution:

    *The Industrial Revolution* by Mary Collins (New York: Children's Press, 2000).

    *The Industrial Revolution* by Robert Ingpen (New York: Chelsea House, 1995).

    *Kids During the Industrial Revolution* by Lisa Wroble (New York: Rosen Publishing, 1999).

# PART 4

# New Directions

## The 20th Century

# March 1917: In a Coffee Shop

## Staging

The five characters can all be seated at a round or rectangular table. If a table is unavailable, five chairs can be placed in a circle. The waitress (Rosie) enters and exits the staging area periodically. The narrator is off to the side and can be standing at a podium or lectern.

Narrator
X

Aunt Carla
X

Angie
X

Uncle Mack
X

Rosie
X

Rupert
X

Martha
X

**NARRATOR:** In 1914, most people believed that a major war would never happen. Yet happen it did. The assassination of Archduke Ferdinand and his wife sparked a conflict between major European countries that was to last for four years. Country sided with country; alliances were formed and war spread across Europe like wildfire.

In the early years of World War I, the United States maintained a position of neutrality. They did supply food, clothing, and ammunition to the Allied forces, but did not send over any troops. It wasn't until February of 1917, when German U-boats sank three American merchant ships that the war hit close to home for many Americans. After the interception of a secret message between Germany and Mexico, the United States declared war on Germany in April 1917. The armed forces were mobilized and thousands of soldiers were sent overseas.

As our play opens it's a Tuesday morning in Los Angeles in late 1917. The sun is just beginning to creep up over the horizon. The day dawns clear and bright as a small band of seagulls glides through the air overhead. The sounds of traffic can be heard in the distance. The city is waking, wiping the slumber from its eyes, and rising to meet the day. Five people have gathered at the Red Roof Diner to share an early morning cup of coffee and some conversation.

**ROSIE:** (*walking to the table with a coffee pot*) You folks want some more coffee?

**AUNT CARLA:** Yeah, how about another refill all around, Rosie.

**ROSIE:** Sure thing. (*pours coffee into each of the cups and then exits*)

**UNCLE MACK:** Say, Rupert, isn't young Joe thinking about joining the Army?

**RUPERT:** Yeah, Little Joe's thinking about it. You know he graduated from high school last year. Seems like he's had a devil of a time trying to find a job. There's plenty of jobs around, but he can't seem to hold on to one long enough. I suppose joining the Army might be a good thing for him. Maybe he'll learn some kind of skill or something. You know . . . something he can do when he gets out.

**AUNT CARLA:** Aren't you afraid about all that stuff taking place over in Europe?

**RUPERT:** That's got nothing to do with joining the Army here. He's probably going to do his basic training up in the Bay Area, then be shipped off to some base in Texas or New Jersey to do his tour of duty. We're not worried about it.

**UNCLE MACK:** I don't know. I was talking with my buddy down at the plant the other day and the way he tells it, it looks like that war might be going on for quite some time.

**NARRATOR:** By 1917 the ground war in Europe had come to a standstill. Most of the fighting was occurring along the western front in northern France. German and French soldiers were dug into long trenches and were facing each other over a "no-man's-land" protected by barbed wire and machine guns. There was no progress either way and casualties were high.

**ANGIE:** I'm just scared for my brother. I mean, Joe and I are pretty close and I don't want him going to some foreign country fighting some war that's got nothing to do with us.

**AUNT CARLA:** Yeah, I'm scared, too, Angie. You know that brother of yours is pretty special to me, too. But, the way I hear it, that conflict over there is just between those Germans and Russians and Serbians and all those other countries. Somebody shot somebody, and somebody else got mad because that person was shot when he shouldn't have been shot, and somebody wanted to prove who was the best or strongest. Before you know it, a bunch of real hotheads get all fired up and there's a war going on. I still don't understand why President Wilson had to declare war because of someone else's troubles.

**MARTHA:** Hey, it isn't our war. But, you know what? We're still sending our boys over there—boys like Little Joe, and Diane's son, and those two boys over on Jackson Street. Yeah, we're still sending kids across the ocean and as much as you or I don't like it we should still be supporting that war effort over here.

**NARRATOR:** As men went off to war, many jobs opened up. For the first time, thousands of women entered the workforce. Thousands of black Americans moved north to seek employment in factories. The federal government set up the War Industries Board to organize American industry. The Food Administration was established to encourage farmers to grow more and citizens to eat less, thus saving food to send to the troops overseas. The Committee on Public Information was initiated to spread favorable news about the war effort. Many sectors of American society were mobilized for the war effort.

**RUPERT:** You know my cousin, Larry, the one who went to that college back in the East somewhere? Well, he says that the good old U.S. has always been a neutral country and should have stayed a neutral country.

**AUNT CARLA:** What's he mean by neutral?

**UNCLE MACK:** Neutral means that a country doesn't get involved with other countries. If those other countries have problems, then those problems aren't our problems.

**MARTHA:** Makes sense to me. (*to waitress*) Hey, Rosie, how about something on top? (*points to coffee cup*)

**ROSIE:** You got it. (*she comes over and refills several cups*)

**AUNT CARLA:** I'm not so sure about all that's happening. I mean, there's been a lot of dying. It doesn't seem so long ago that Billy Murdock, you know, the kid that Little Joe used to go to school with, came home in a body bag. Terrible thing . . . I mean that whole family was torn up. Mrs. Murdock never left her house and Mr. Murdock couldn't go to work any more. They haven't been the same since. Losing their only boy to some far distant war. It just didn't make any sense.

**MARTHA:** Yeah, that's what scares me. There have been lots of boys getting shot at, so many boys injured or dying. Hey, Little Joe's our youngest boy. I don't want to have to go down to the train station and pick him up, you know, pick him up in a . . . (*trails off*)

**NARRATOR:** Between the time the United States entered the war in April 1917 and the end of the war in November 1918, over 100,000 soldiers and sailors died in the fighting. During the entire length of the war, from 1914 to 1918, nearly 13 million Europeans were killed.

**ANGIE:** Hey, has anybody heard about that new kind of boat the Germans are using all around the North Atlantic? Some kind of boat that goes underwater and fires torpedoes at ships and stuff.

**RUPERT:** Yeah, I heard they were called U-boats. I guess because they are "underwater boats." Yeah, "submarines" is what I think they were called in the paper. Seems like those Germans just want to sink everything that sails across the ocean, no matter who it belongs to or what country it comes from.

**UNCLE MACK:** Hey, what about that luxury liner from England . . . what did they call it?

**AUNT CARLA:** (*reflective*) Wasn't that the *Lusitania*?

**RUPERT:** Those poor people. Lots of men, women, and children were killed when that ship went down.

**NARRATOR:** The German U-boats were a new weapon of war. They were used to sink military vessels as well as civilian ships. In the early part of the war, the Germans set up a war zone around Great Briton and announced that any ship sailing into the area was subject to attack. They went on to say that they could not guarantee the safety of the ships of any neutral nations. On May 7, 1915, a German U-boat sank the British passenger ship *Lusitania*. More than 1,000 people, including 128 Americans, lost their lives. The Germans targeted that ship because they suspected that it was carrying bombs and ammunition.

**UNCLE MACK:** Yeah, it sure is a scary time.

**MARTHA:**    You know, I was just thinking. Remember what they were saying all during the election in 1916? The Democrats kept pushing for reelecting President Wilson because of that slogan—"He kept us out of war."

**AUNT CARLA:**    I remember that. It seemed to be a big deal with them.

**UNCLE MACK:**    Yeah, but then look what happened. Those darned U-boats started sinking a whole bunch of ships all over the darned ocean.

**RUPERT:**    Boy, did that get a lot of people upset. But, you know what really burned the president was that deal that Germany made with Mexico. Remember that?

**MARTHA:**    Yeah, I sure do. It was some kind of secret note that some spies had gotten hold of. Yeah, it was some note that said . . . what was it now? Oh, yeah, seems like the Germans were going to give Arizona, New Mexico, and Texas to Mexico if the Mexicans declared war on the U.S.

**RUPERT:**    Boy, did that raise some stink!

**UNCLE MACK:**    You're not kidding. Those congressmen in Washington were running around like a bunch of headless chickens when they found that one out. I'll tell you, President Wilson sure did have steam pouring out of his head. And the senators . . . remember them? They were shouting and screaming and making a fuss all over the place.

**RUPERT:**    Sure is scary.

**MARTHA:**    Yeah, I'm just plain worried. I'm worried about my boy and I'm worried about this country. Don't know what to think.

**AUNT CARLA:**    Rosie, how 'bout one more for the road?

**ROSIE:**    Okay.

**NARRATOR:**    World War I was known as "the war to end all wars." By the time World War I ended on November 11, 1918, the war had affected many countries and millions of people. Germany accepted responsibility for the war and agreed to pay $33 billion in damages to the Allies. Germany also gave up their claims to important industrial regions. Several new European nations were created from territory that once belonged to the defeated countries. In a span of four years the world had changed dramatically. It was the end of one era and the beginning of a new one.

## Possible Extensions

1.  Invite students to discuss reasons why World War I was referred to as "the war to end all wars." What were the implications of that statement?

2.  Invite students to create their own readers theatre script about American soldiers going over to Europe to fight in World War I. What kind of discussions would the soldiers be having?

3.  Encourage students to create maps of Europe with significant World War I battles recorded on the maps. What were some of the most important conflicts during the war? Where did these occur?

4.  Divide the class into two groups. One group is supportive of America's entry into World War I and the other group opposes America's entry into the war. Invite the groups to conduct a debate on the pros and cons of each position.

5.  Students may wish to obtain additional information about World War I. The following Web sites can provide them with important data:

    http://campus.northpark.edu/history//WebChron/World/WWI.html

    http://www.worldwar1.com

    http://www.pbs.org/greatwar/

    http://www.mrdowling.com/706wars.html

6.  Peter Bosco's *World War I* (America at War Series) (New York: Facts on File, 1991) offers students reasons for America's participation in World War I and the war's significance for the country.

# A Right to Vote

## Staging

The characters can all be standing or seated on tall stools. The narrator is positioned to the side of the staging area at a podium or lectern.

|  |  |
|---|---|
| Father | Mother |
| X | X |
| Daughter | Son |
| X | X |

Narrator

X

**NARRATOR:**  In 1870 the 15th Amendment to the U.S. Constitution was passed. This amendment stated that states could not deny the right to vote to any citizen because of race or color. In effect, this amendment gave blacks the right to vote for the first time in our country's history. After the 15th Amendment was passed, many women became angry because they had not been guaranteed the right to vote. In 1890, Wyoming became the first state to allow women to vote. By 1920, 15 states, mostly in the West had given this right to women. Nevertheless, up until 1920, women in this country could not vote in any federal election. Men could vote, but their wives could not.

For years, various groups around the country advocated a woman's right to vote. This movement, referred to as women's suffrage, attempted to gain women full voting privileges. There was much argument and much divisiveness about this issue.

**SON:** What is this women's suffrage? How did it begin?

**FATHER:** It actually began in 1848 in Seneca Falls, New York. Two women named Lucretia Mott and Elizabeth Cady Stanton called a convention in that town. Several men and women attended the convention and declared that women should have equal rights in education, property, voting, and other matters. The conventioneers believed that the framers of the Declaration of Independence had intentionally forgotten women in demanding rights for the citizens of the new country.

**DAUGHTER:** What did these conventioneers hope to accomplish?

**MOTHER:** They believed that if women gained the right to vote, then they would also be able to gain other rights as well.

**DAUGHTER:** I don't get it. A woman's place is in the home. She should be taking care of the kids, cleaning the house, and looking after her husband.

**FATHER:** Your one-sided view assumes that women are less intelligent than men, that they can't make decisions, that they can't think for themselves.

**SON:** Why should they think? What do they need to think about? Providing for the needs of their husbands is all they need to worry about, and that certainly doesn't take a lot of intelligence.

**MOTHER:** Do you really believe that every woman is less intelligent than her husband? Do you really believe that all men are smart?

SON:    Every man in this country makes important decisions every day. We make political decisions, we make economic decisions, we make commercial decisions. Certainly we can make decisions for our wives. Why should they worry their pretty little heads over affairs of state or the distribution of goods and services?

NARRATOR:    There was a mistaken belief that the women's suffrage movement was supported entirely by women and challenged entirely by men. Such was not the case. Many men were attracted to the movement because they felt that it would democratize voting in this country. Several women opposed the movement because it upset the status quo. Interestingly, this movement was accepted by both men and women as much as it was challenged by both men and women.

FATHER:    You're worried that women are actually smarter than you! You're worried that women will show you up in the political arena! You think men have all the answers just because they have all the control.

DAUGHTER:    Hey, hold on a minute. What's the big deal? Why vote? (to Mother) Aren't you satisfied with your life right now? Aren't all your needs provided for by Father? Aren't you happy and content with what you have?

MOTHER:    (forcefully) But, women ARE equal, with equal intelligence AND equal skills at judging a situation AND understanding the politics of a situation. Certainly, you can't argue the fact that women have a right to participate in laws that are going to affect them.

SON:    Let's talk history. For years, indeed for centuries, women have gotten along just fine without any so-called right to vote. They've been fed and cared for and provided for and so on. Their main job is to take care of the family; men's main job is to provide for that family. And one of the ways a family is provided for is through the political process—a process in which elected officials are put in office to enact the laws that protect us all. For centuries that's been done by men. Why should it change now?

**FATHER:** It's simple. Women contribute equally in society and raise the children who will be the leaders of the next generation. That gives them the right to vote . . . and to have full participation in that society. Are you afraid that women's participation in politics will lead to the end of family life?

**SON:** Well, won't it? Women have a full-time job at home. Why would they ever want to take on more responsibilities outside the home? If they did, something would suffer. And the thing that would suffer most would be the family.

**MOTHER:** Are you afraid of losing your power? Are you afraid of losing your influence? Are you afraid that by granting women full suffrage your manhood will be diminished.

**DAUGHTER:** We're not afraid of anything. We just don't think women need to vote. What's the point? Voting has been and should always be a man's privilege.

**FATHER:** Perhaps you're blind to progress and blind to the social conditions of the early twentieth century.

**SON:** I just don't see the need for women to do something they're not prepared to do, not ready to do, and not qualified to do.

**MOTHER:** What you may not see is equality. What you may not see is the fact that women are just as smart, just as intelligent, and just as capable at making their own decisions as are men. What you may not see is what's right around the corner: the fact that women throughout this country will be given the right to vote. And with that vote, they will have such a profound influence that the American political landscape will be altered forever.

**NARRATOR:** On June 4, 1919, the U.S. Congress voted to add the 19th Amendment to the U.S. Constitution. Over the next year the amendment was ratified by the necessary 36 states. On August 26, 1920, the 19th Amendment became national law. That amendment reads as follows: "The rights of citizens of the United States to vote shall not be denied or abridged by the United States or by any state on account of sex. Congress shall have power to enforce this article by appropriate legislation."

Women were able to exercise their newfound voting rights in the national election of 1920. Since then, women have traditionally voted in larger percentages than have men, often determining the outcomes of many elections at the federal and state levels. Women are, and continue to be, a potent force in American politics.

## Possible Extensions

1. A very interesting article about how one man (and his mother) ultimately decided the fate of the 19th Amendment can be found at http://www.blueshoenashville.com/suffragehistory.html.

2. Invite students to discuss how the American political landscape has been changed by women. How did women affect the most recent presidential election?

3. Encourage students to obtain information (via library or Internet resources) on the women in their city, county, or state who hold political office. Students may wish to create special bulletin board displays of these women.

4. Invite students to create their own readers theatre script about giving 18-year-olds the right to vote. They may wish to pattern their "arguments" on those offered in the script above.

5. Students may wish to investigate the biographies of leaders in the women's suffrage movement. People to investigate include Lucretia Mott, Elizabeth Cady Stanton, Susan B. Anthony, Lucy Stone, Carrie Chapman Catt, Maud Wood Park, Lucy Burns, Alice Paul, and Harriet E. Blatch.

6. Students may be interested in a chronology of events about women's suffrage worldwide. They can read a timeline of those events at http://www.ipu.org/wmn-e/suffrage.htm. Invite students to note that there are still two countries in the world that do not extend voting privileges to women.

# A Bowl of Soup, a Piece of Bread

## Staging

The narrator can sit on a stool on the side of the staging area. Behind a table, the other characters can be standing in line in back of three characters who have no speaking parts.

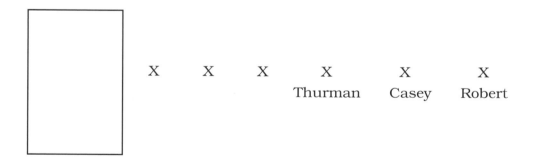

X    X    X    X    X    X
                Thurman  Casey  Robert

Narrator
X

**NARRATOR:** It is the fall of 1933. Millions of people have lost their jobs, banks have closed, stocks are worthless; it is the height of the Depression. Many cities have set up soup kitchens and bread lines to keep people from starving. Those that are working are selling apples or shining shoes just to get

**113**

a few pennies to pay the rent or buy food for the family. Many people are homeless and sleeping on park benches and in alleyways.

Men who once had good-paying jobs spend their days standing in line. This scene takes place in a soup kitchen somewhere in Chicago. Three men are waiting for a bowl of soup and a piece of bread.

**THURMAN:** (*frustrated*) I'm really getting tired of spending my time standing in line waiting for someone to give me a luke-warm bowl of bad soup and a couple of pieces of stale bread. This is humiliating.

**CASEY:** (*sadly*) You think you've got it bad, pal. Why, last year, my wife and three children and I had to spend the winter under a piece of canvas in the park. We slept on sheets of old cardboard I'd found in an alley somewhere and the blankets we used were the clothes on our back. Man, that was one tough winter.

**NARRATOR:** At the height of the Depression, about 1 million people became drifters. They would go from city to city looking for any type of work at all. Many would do anything for a job. Families were frequently split up, so that various family members could take the few jobs available in different locations. Two hundred thousand children were left to fend for themselves—their families unable to take care of them.

**ROBERT:** Yeah, I guess we all got it pretty bad. Why, just three months ago I worked in a big office building. Had a good job, too. Made good money. Why, the missus and I were planning to take a vacation to California to see her sister. Yeah, her sister lives right there in L.A. Right there where it's nice and warm, and the sun shines all day long. Right there in the land of milk and honey.

**THURMAN:** I hate to break it to you, buddy, but there is no land of milk and honey. This is the Great Depression. You know, the Great Depression that has hit every man, woman and child in this country. It doesn't make any difference where you live. You can live right here in the Windy City, you can live in the middle of Kansas, you can live right on the beach in Miami, or you can live right on the shores of Southern California. It makes no difference whatsoever where you live. You are still going to be in the Great Depression.

**CASEY:** Yeah, I suppose you're right. I mean, just look around. What do you see? You see other poor slobs just like us standing in line, waiting for some soup and some bread. Good guys. Good guys just like you and me . . . standing in line. Look at them. (*points*) They were just like us. Good jobs, good homes, good lives . . . everything to live for and then this. Everything gone belly-up. Everything's gone sour. Can't believe it. I just can't believe it!

**ROBERT:** It doesn't seem like it's ever going end, does it? Seems like it's going to go on and on. Oh, I know, Mr. Roosevelt is trying to do his best. He's trying to create some jobs and projects around the country to give guys like us some work . . . some work to pay the bills . . . some work to keep our families together. But, maybe, it's just not enough. Oh, sure, he's doing his best, but it's just not enough.

**NARRATOR:** President Roosevelt swept into office on the promise of a "new deal" for all Americans. This meant the establishment of a number of government programs. These programs aimed to restore the shattered economy, give a new sense of purpose to the federal government, and restore the faith of the American people. Some of the programs and proposals included the Tennessee Valley Authority, which regulated water use in parts of the South; the Agricultural Adjustment Act, which dealt with the problem of low farm prices; the Works Progress Administration, which provided public jobs for the unemployed; and the National Youth Administration, which offered employment to individuals between the ages of 16 and 25.

**THURMAN:** My whole life I've been working hard just to put a few crumbs on the table. My whole life I've been working and now this . . . now this. What am I going to do? My wife and I have three kids and another kid on the way. What am I going to do?

**CASEY:** Maybe we should go out to that land of plenty in California. At least we'd be warm. At least we wouldn't have to worry about not having enough heat for the winter. At least we wouldn't have that worry hanging over our heads.

**ROBERT:** Yeah, sounds like a plan. Except for one thing.

**THURMAN:** What's that?

**ROBERT:** How are we going to get there? It's going to take money to get there. Heck, we don't even have enough money to buy one stupid meal. Look at us. Look at us standing in this line waiting for some poor soul to give us some stale bread and lukewarm soup just so we can make it through another day. No, my friends, I'm afraid the Golden State just isn't in the picture for us.

**CASEY:** I suppose you're right.

**THURMAN:** So what do we do? There's no work, there are no jobs, there isn't anything at all.

**ROBERT:** There sure seems to be a lot of nothing around here lately. Seems to be a lot of nothing all over the country, too. No money, no banks, no jobs . . . yes sir, just a lot of nothing everywhere you look, everywhere you go.

**CASEY:** It's got to get better, guys, it's just got to get better.

**THURMAN:** You'd think so, wouldn't you? You'd think it couldn't get any worse than it has already. You'd think we'd be on the bottom of the barrel now. You'd think we hit rock bottom. But, some days, it just seems to get worse than the day before. It just seems to get worse each day you wake up.

**CASEY:** Yeah, I guess you're right. I sure do hope Mr. Roosevelt knows what he's doing.

**ROBERT:** So do I. I don't know how much longer I can do this. I just don't know.

**THURMAN:**   Yeah, me too. Hey, looks like I'm next for some soup. Hey, it's got some meat in it. This soup doesn't look so bad after all.

**NARRATOR:**   Roosevelt's New Deal was not without its controversies. Various agencies and policies were challenged in the courts. But, for the most part, the federal government was able to enact several reforms including assistance for farmers, support for labor, passage of the Social Security Act, banking and utility reforms, and a modification in the tax system. What emerged from this period of American history was increased responsibilities of the federal government in economic and social welfare.

## Possible Extensions

1.  If possible, invite students to interview their parents or grandparents. What stories have they heard about the Great Depression? Do they know anyone who lived during that time?

2.  Invite students to investigate library resources on the Dust Bowl of the 1930s. Small groups, of students may wish to create their own readers theatre script on the life of a family living in the Dust Bowl.

3.  The following Internet resources can provide students with valuable information about the Great Depression of the 1930s:

    http://www.bbc.co.uk/education/modern/

    http://www.pbs.org/wgbh/amex/rails

4.  The following Web sites offer extensive information about the Dust Bowl:

    http://drylands.nasm.edu:1995/dust.html

    http://www.pbs.org/wgbh/amex/dustbowl/

    http://www.discovery.com/area/history/dustbowl/
       dustbowlopener.html.

5.  Invite students to write an imaginary letter of hope to a family living through the Great Depression of the 1930s. What encouragement or support would they want to offer the family? What would they like to say to them? Plan sufficient time to discuss various letters.

# December 7, 1941: Aboard the USS Arizona

## Staging

The narrator is off to one side of the staging area, preferably unseen by the audience. Each of the characters wanders on to the staging area and says his piece. After speaking, each character sits down in a chair near the front of the staging area. The characters do not talk to each other (or acknowledge each other). They speak only to the audience. For added effect, you may wish to play sound effects of dive-bombing airplanes in the background. These can be made by playing a video of a World War II movie and recording the airplane sequences on audiotape. If this is not possible, invite some students beforehand to make their own sound effects of diving airplanes (for about five minutes) and record those sounds on audiotape for playback during the presentation.

```
Narrator                                                              Paul
    X                                              Tommy        X
                                          Dean        X
                                 Prichard      X
                         Digger      X
                 Mason      X
          Terry     X
            X
                                               (chairs)
                                         X    X    X    X
                                            X    X    X
```

**NARRATOR:** (*calmly, then excitedly*) The morning dawned bright and clear. Sunlight sparkled on the water, palm trees arched over expanses of beach, and families arose—to get ready for church on another Sunday morning in Hawaii. It was just another day in paradise.

The surprise came from overhead. Attacking planes swept over Pearl Harbor at 7:55 A.M., dropping bombs on the columns of battleships moored along "Battleship Row." One of those battleships was the *USS Arizona.* Ten minutes after the beginning of the attack, a bomb crashes through the decks of the *Arizona* and explodes in its magazine—the place where all its ammunition is stored. A thunderous explosion rips the ship's sides open like a tin can. The blast sweeps over the ship in a horrific inferno—a fire that engulfs everything in its wake.

**PAUL:** (*dazed*) I never saw it coming. I never saw them. I was getting some grub for breakfast and I never saw them. They came in too fast. One minute it was quiet and the next minute there was noise and crying and noise and fire all around. I never saw it, I never saw it, I never saw it. Loud noises. Lots of noise everywhere. Noise all over the place—airplanes, explosions, fire—noise all over the place. I never saw them coming. Where did they come from? Where did they come from? Where did they . . . ?

**NARRATOR:** Men are running everywhere. Bodies are littering the decks. Some are alive; others are barely clinging to the few shreds of life they still have. Confusion reigns as explosion after explosion tears through the ship. Blood-curdling screams and the stench of death are everywhere. Panic fills the air as the once majestic ship begins to sink into the harbor. Within minutes 1,300 lives will go down with their ship. One sailor stumbles across the deck talking to no one in particular.

**TOMMY:** (*frantic and confused*) Oh, my gosh, oh my gosh. Look at this. Just look at this. Oh, my gosh, oh my gosh. There are bodies everywhere. Just look at them. Young kids, just a bunch of lousy young kids. Kids from Kansas City. Kids from San Francisco. Kids from states like Wisconsin or Tennessee or Arizona. Just a bunch of kids. Kids with moms and dads and sisters and kid brothers and aunts and uncles and grandmothers and. . . . Oh, my gosh, these poor kids—young kids, dead kids; young and dead. That's what they are now—young and dead. Kids with their whole lives before them—girlfriends and wives and their own children and houses and cars. . . . Oh, look at them. These kids are dead. These kids will never have wives or children or cars or anything. These kids have nothing . . . nothing at all. Look at them, just look at them. They're just a bunch of young dead kids . . . no future . . . no future . . . (*trailing off*) no future . . . no future . . .

**NARRATOR:** Overhead another squadron of planes dives out of the sky. Machine guns are piercing the air with their rat-a-tat-tat. Bombs are dropping everywhere. It seems as though the entire sky is on fire. Smoke is pouring out of gaping holes in the bulkheads. An endless succession of screams pierces the air. Near the stern of the ship a young sailor, clothes in tatters, stumbles across the deck.

**DEAN:** (*crying and sobbing*) Marty, Marty, Marty. Where are you, man? Where are you? Don't leave me now. You're my best buddy . . . my best buddy. Don't leave me, man. Hey, we had so much fun together. You can't leave me now. Don't leave me. Remember that night in the hotel in Honolulu? Remember when we both put on grass skirts and danced around the lobby? Remember what the manager did to us? Remember how everyone looked at us? Yeah, those were some good times, pal. Don't leave me, now. Don't leave me. You can't leave me. You can't leave me.

NARRATOR: The dead and wounded are everywhere. Most are caught below decks, but a few manage to crawl, creep, or swim away from the dying ship. A few manage to make it to shore where sailors from other ships find them and carry them to the nearest infirmary or hospital. The dead and dying are everywhere. Some were lucky; most were not.

PRICHARD: (*calmly, yet stunned*) I'll never forget that explosion. There I was, sitting on my bunk, putting on my shoes when it came. I didn't have a battle station, so I didn't know where to go. I figured something was wrong. You just don't have some explosion at 8:00 every Sunday morning. So I ran to the port door leading to the quarterdeck and went outside. Bombs were dropping all over the place and our own anti-aircraft guns were firing up into the skies. I could see some of the planes off in the distance. There were fires and explosions everywhere. When I reached the boat deck, the mast exploded and shrapnel and fragments whizzed all around me. Why I never got hit I'll never know. As I ran aft I tripped over something. There were two seaman first class lying on the deck, arms around each other, both dead, both holding on to each other for support and comfort. Everywhere I looked there were burned bodies. I couldn't stand it. I also knew that the ship was doomed. I don't know what it was or how it happened, but the next thing I knew I was in the water. I guess the concussion from some explosion knocked me overboard. The shore looked far away, but I had to swim. So, I swam. I swam past some bodies. I just kept swimming for the shore. It looked so far away, so far away, so far away, but I just kept swimming. I must have passed out 'cause the next thing I knew I was in the infirmary with bandages around my head and a sling on my arm. I guess I was one of the lucky ones . . . just one of the lucky ones.

NARRATOR: More planes race down from the clouds and spray the ship with a hail of gunfire. Another wave of bombs falls across the decks twisting metals and scattering debris in a thousand different directions. The dead are mounting. Death is everywhere. All around there are dead sailors. Most of them are kids, not even old enough to vote.

**DIGGER:** (*without emotion, in a ghost-like trance*) I never made it. I never knew what hit us. One minute I was playing cards with Four Eyes, Crusher, and Mason and the next minute I was gone. Just like that, I was gone. Nineteen years old . . . my first tour of duty . . . in beautiful Hawaii . . . and just like that, I was gone. What's going to happen? What's going to happen to my mother, to my father, to my sister Maggie? What's going to happen to them now that I'm gone? What's going to happen to Betty Sue, my girl back home? We had such big plans, such big plans. We were going to get married and have a house and maybe some kids. What's going to happen to her now that I'm gone? What's going to happen to everybody now that I'm gone? What will they do? I never saw it coming. Just like that, I was gone.

**NARRATOR:** The Japanese Zeros drop more bombs on more ships. Some are completely destroyed, others are mangled and ripped apart, and a few are still seaworthy. But the destruction is extensive; everywhere there are clouds of smoke and a hundred different fires. The noise and the smell are overpowering. Emotions are high and fear leads to anger in those that survived the bombardment.

**MASON:** (*angry*) One minute he's there. The next minute he's not. (*shaking his fist*) Listen, you dirty little so-and-so's. You killed him. You killed my buddy. You just dropped some stupid bombs and killed my buddy. Who do you think you are! My buddy's dead . . . he's dead . . . my buddy's dead! (*breaking down and sobbing*)

**NARRATOR:** Planes, ships, and human lives are forever lost. One sailor, one lucky sailor, who miraculously survives the inferno on the *USS Arizona* sums it up this way:

**TERRY:** (*defiant*) Look at this, just look at this (*sweeps his arm*). In two hours eight battleships were damaged or destroyed. In two hours, 188 planes were completely destroyed. In two hours 2,403 people were killed. In two hours, in two lousy, stinking hours, lives were lost and lives were changed. In two hours a nation was changed. In two hours a war was launched and an army was mobilized. In two hours the fate of a nation and the fate of a world were forever altered. In just two hours everything changed. In just two hours I lost my best friend. In just two hours I lost most of the crew I sailed with. In just two hours I lost my right leg and my youth. In just two hours I was changed. In just two hours. In just two lousy, stinking hours.

**NARRATOR:**   December 7, 1941, was called "a day that would live in infamy" by President Roosevelt. It was only 24 hours after the Japanese attack on Pearl Harbor that the U.S. Congress declared war on Japan. That declaration was signed by President Roosevelt and the United States was propelled into World War II. One day later, both Italy and Germany, as partners with Japan, declared war on the United States. The world changed dramatically. And the world still remembers that sunny Sunday morning in Hawaii in 1941.

# Possible Extensions

1.  Invite students to take on the role of various fictitious sailors on board the *USS Arizona* on December 7, 1941. Encourage students to write letters back home describing some of the events and circumstances of December 7, 1941.

2.  The *USS Arizona* Memorial in Pearl Harbor is one of the most striking and moving monuments in the country. Invite students to log on to gather information about this monument at http://www.nps.gov/usar/.

3.  Invite students to write a readers theatre script centering on the events that may have taken place on the mainland of the United States when people first heard the news about the bombing of Pearl Harbor.

4.  Invite students to discuss why President Roosevelt said that December 7, 1941 was "a day of infamy."

5.  Students may be interested in viewing a movie about the bombing of Pearl Harbor. A film such as *Tora, Tora, Tora* might be appropriate to show students. Encourage students to discuss how the events of that day changed the course of history.

# December 1, 1955: Montgomery, Alabama

## Staging

Students are arranged in two rows of four chairs each. The chairs are set up to look like the interior of a bus. One chair is separate from the others and simulates the bus driver's seat. Two chairs in the back are empty. Man 1 is standing throughout the performance; all other characters are seated. The narrator is placed at a podium or lectern at the rear of the staging area.

|  |  |  |  | Narrator |
|---|---|---|---|---|
|  |  |  |  | X |
| Man 2 | Woman 1 | Man 4 | (seat) |  |
| X | X | X | X |  |
| Man 1 |  |  |  |  |
| X |  |  |  |  |
| Bus Driver | Rosa | Man 3 | Woman 2 | (seat) |
| X | X | X | X | X |

**NARRATOR:** The year is 1955. The United States is enjoying renewed prosperity after the Second World War. Industries are growing, new homes are being built, and there are plenty of jobs for people who wanted them. This new prosperity means a booming economy and new freedoms.

However, not everyone enjoys the same freedoms. Black Americans face discrimination in these post-war years, just as they have at other times in our nation's history. Blacks cannot eat in many restaurants. They cannot attend the same schools as white children. In many ways, blacks do not have the same civil rights as whites.

In some cities, particularly in the South, there are laws that discriminate against blacks. These laws, called "Jim Crow" laws, force black people to be segregated from white people. They are in place even though not all whites believe blacks are second-class citizens. One law in Montgomery, Alabama forces black people to ride in the back of city buses; only white people can sit in the front of a bus.

The date is December 1, 1955. Rosa Parks, a black woman, is on her way home from work in Montgomery, Alabama. She boards a city bus, pays her fare, and sits down in one of the few remaining seats. Let's look in at this fictionalized account of one of the pivotal events in the civil rights movement.

**ROSA:** (*to no one in particular*) Whew! I'm tired. That was sure a tough day at work. I'm just plain tired. Dog tired.

**WOMAN 2:** (*to Man 4*) Did you see that? (*pointing at Rosa*) Did you see what that black woman just did?

**MAN 4:** Yeah, that black woman just sat down in the front of the bus.

**WOMAN 1:** (*indignant*) Hey, just who does she think she is? Doesn't she know she can't do that. She just can't do that. It's against the law!

**MAN 3:** Yeah, doesn't she know those are white seats? Blacks can't sit in those seats. Those are white seats.

**MAN 4:** (*calling to Rosa*) Hey, black woman, you can't sit there. Don't you know that's a white seat? Only white folks can sit there.

**ROSA:** (*ignoring the last comment*) Boy, am I tired. I just want to get home and put up my old tired feet.

**MAN 2:** (*to Rosa*) Hey, lady, you can't sit there. Blacks are supposed to be in the back of the bus. Don't you know blacks are supposed to be in the back of the bus?

**ROSA:** Yeah, I know that. But I'm tired and I'm gonna sit here.

**MAN 1:** (*entering the bus*) Hey lady, you're in my seat.

**ROSA:** (*slightly agitated*) No, this here is my seat. I'm sitting down in this seat. I'm tired and I just want to get home and I'm sitting down in this seat on this bus and I'm going home.

**BUS DRIVER:** Hey, lady, there's a law and the law says that blacks have to sit back there. (*points to the back*) Look, there are two seats back there. Why don't you just get up and go sit back in your section of the bus?

**ROSA:** I'm not getting up. I sat here and I'm staying here. This is my seat and I want to go home.

**MAN 1:** (*angry*) Lady, how many times do you have to be told? You should know the law: blacks in the back and whites in the front. That's how it is. That's the way it's always been and that's the way it's going to always be.

**MAN 3:** He's right, lady. The law's the law. You'd better get your black self out of that seat and sit back there.

**WOMAN 2:** You'd better move lady. You're going to cause more trouble than it's worth. The law was made for a reason.

**BUS DRIVER:** Lady, look. I ain't movin' this bus until you get up out of that seat and move to the back. That's the law and you got to obey the law.

**ROSA:** That may be the law, but that don't mean that the law is right. I'm just another person on the bus. Another person like you and you and you. (*points to several people*) I'm just a person who wants to go home. Whether I sit here or whether I sit back there makes no difference to anyone. We all get to the same place at the same time, so it makes no difference where we sit. Everything's the same.

**WOMAN 1:**   (*standing up*) Hey, the law says you got to sit back there. (*points*) So why don't you move yourself back there just like every other black person's supposed to do!

**MAN 4:**   Look, you probably noticed that this bus ain't moving. The law says you sit back there. When you sit back there then we can move.

**MAN 1:**   I'm getting real impatient. You're sitting in a white seat. I'm a white man and I want my seat.

**BUS DRIVER:**   Look, lady, I ain't goin' to move this bus one inch until you get to the back.

**MAN 4:**   Come on, how 'bout movin' it?

**WOMAN 1:**   (*angry*) Hey, you, you're breakin' the law. You should be arrested.

**WOMAN 2:**   (*indignant*) I ain't never seen anything like this. Just who does she think she is? Hmmmmf, a black woman sittin' in a white man's seat. Yup, she should just be arrested and hauled off the jail.

**MAN 1:**   (*impatient*) I'm waiting. You gonna move or not?

**BUS DRIVER:**   (*demanding*) Lady, you've got one more chance. Either you get yourself out of this man's seat or I'm goin' to have to call the cops. You understand?

**ROSA:**   Yeah, I understand. I understand that I sat down in this seat first. I understand that I'm tired and I want to go home. I understand that there are some seats back there for this man to sit in. I understand that it's time to get this bus going so that we can all get home. That's what I understand.

**MAN 3:**   What you don't understand is that you're breaking the law. And the law was made for a reason. Blacks in the back. That's the law. (*to everyone*) Ain't that right, folks?

**EVERYONE:**   Yeah!

**MAN 1:**   You movin', lady?

**ROSA:**   I'm staying right here. I'm not moving.

**BUS DRIVER:**   Then I got no choice. I'm callin' the cops.

**NARRATOR:**   The police arrive and arrest Rosa Parks for breaking the law. To protest, the Reverend Martin Luther King Jr. organizes a boycott of the Montgomery, Alabama bus system. During the boycott blacks throughout the city do not ride city buses. Instead, they walk or take other forms of transportation. Because most of the bus riders in Montgomery are black, this boycott has a severe economic impact on the bus system, which almost goes out of business. After several months, the owners finally agree to integrate the city bus system.

The success of the boycott led to mass protests in support of the civil rights of blacks. Rosa Parks lost her job as a seamstress as a result of the protest, but in 1956 the Supreme Court of the United States ruled that the bus company had denied black bus riders their civil rights.

Rosa Park's refusal to give up her seat was a pivotal point in the struggle for equal rights. It was a statement that everyone should be guaranteed the same rights and privileges regardless of color. Rosa Park's simple act was a lightning rod for the civil rights movement—a movement that forever changed the face of American society. Her determination and bravery have been celebrated in songs and books and she has been the recipient of many awards. And all she did was stand up for what she knew was right.

## Possible Extensions

1.  Invite students to investigate other "Jim Crow" laws that were in effect in several Southern states. Why were these laws enacted? How were they enforced?

2.  Invite students to discuss laws or rules that may discriminate against young people. For example, not being able to enter a movie because of its rating; not being able to purchase a book or CD because of certain words or lyrics; not being able to purchase items such as cigarettes or liquor. How do students feel about those laws?

3.  Students may be interested in learning more about the life of Rosa Parks. The following Web sites are particularly instructive:

    http://www.galegroup.com/schools/freresrc/blkhstry/parksros.htm

    http://www.greatwomen.org/parks.htm

    http://www.health.org/gpower/girlarea/gpguests/RosaParks.htm

    http://www.grandtimes.com/Rosa.html

4.  Students can learn more about the Montgomery Bus Boycott at the following sites:

    http://www.holidays.net/mlk/rosa.htm

    http://campus.northpark.edu/history/WebChron/USA/
       MontBus.html

5.  Encourage students to create a readers theatre script about one or more events in the civil rights movement. Which events were pivotal? Who were some of the civil rights leaders in the 1950s and 1960s?

6.  Here are some children's books about Rosa Parks that you may wish to share with your students:

    *Dear Mrs. Parks: A Dialogue with Today's Youth* by Rosa Parks and Gregory J. Reed (New York: Lee and Low, 1996).

    *I Am Rosa Parks* by Rosa Parks and James Haskins (New York: Dial, 1997).

    *If a Bus Could Talk: The Story of Rosa Parks* by Faith Ringgold (New York: Simon & Schuster, 1999).

    *A Picture Book of Rosa Parks* by David A. Adler (New York: Holiday House, 1993).

    *Rosa Parks* by Eloise Greenfield (New York: HarperCollins, 1996).

# PART 5

# Recent History, Recent Challenges

## The 20th and 21st Centuries

# Eight Days, Three Hours, and Eighteen Minutes

## Staging

All the characters are news reporters. They can be seated facing the audience on chairs or stools. Each should be behind a desk, table, or music stand. If possible, a fake microphone (made from construction paper) can be placed in front of each reporter. The narrator should be offstage and out of sight of the audience. The "off-stage voice" also should be unseen.

Narrator
  X

          Reporter 1        Reporter 2        Reporter 3
             X                X              X

                                                    Offstage Voice

**NARRATOR:** Throughout the 1960s the United States was engaged in a "space race" with the Soviet Union. Each wanted to be the first to land men on the Moon. Millions of dollars were invested in the space program. Manned space travel in the United States was spearheaded by the Mercury Project (one man in a space capsule), the Gemini Project (two men in a space capsule), and the Apollo Program (three men in a space capsule). Each rocket launch and each space capsule orbit of the earth added to our knowledge about space travel.

The cost of space exploration grew to billions of dollars. Many Americans in the late 1960s were critical of the amount of money that was spent on the space program. But that criticism was temporarily quieted when the United States sent three astronauts on a history-making voyage to the Moon.

The date is July 16, 1969. There are clear skies over Cape Kennedy, Florida as *Apollo 11* is poised on the launch pad for one of the most historic flights in aviation history—indeed, one of the most historic voyages in the history of mankind. (*pause*)

9:32 A.M., eastern standard time.

**REPORTER 1:**   Apollo 11 has just left the launch pad. In 11 minutes it will reach an altitude of over 120 miles and a speed of 17,400 miles per hour.

**REPORTER 2:**   Soon afterward, the first two stages of the Saturn V rocket will drop away and fall into the Atlantic Ocean.

**REPORTER 3:**   In less than three hours, the third stage will ignite and propel the spacecraft on a direct course for the earth's only satellite, Moon, nearly 230,000 miles away.

**NARRATOR:**   12:49 P.M.

**REPORTER 1:**   The spacecraft is traveling at a speed of 24,300 miles per hours now.

**REPORTER 2:**   Now the *Apollo* crew must perform the first of several critical maneuvers. They must separate *Columbia* from the rest of the spacecraft and reverse position in order to dock head to head with the *Eagle*, still inside the spacecraft. (*long pause*) They did it! *Eagle* and *Columbia* have now separated from the third stage of the rocket and are on their way to the Moon.

**NARRATOR:**   12:58 A.M., July 19, 1969: three days later.

**REPORTER 3:**   *Apollo* is now closing in on the Moon. The three astronauts have been monitoring their spacecraft making sure everything is in complete working order.

**REPORTER 1:**   Two hundred miles above the surface of the Moon, the captain gives the order to fire the rockets in order to slow the spacecraft to a speed of 3,600 miles per hour.

**REPORTER 2:**   The *Apollo* spacecraft has been captured by lunar gravity and enters an orbit 60 miles above the surface of the Moon.

**NARRATOR:**   1:46 P.M., July 20, 1969.

**REPORTER 3:**   After 14 orbits around the Moon, the *Eagle*, with the two astronauts Neil Armstrong and Buzz Aldrin inside, separates from *Columbia.*

**NARRATOR:**   3:08 P.M.

**REPORTER 1:**   The *Eagle*'s landing gear has just been released. Aldrin and Armstrong are making their descent to the surface of the Moon.

**REPORTER 2:**   The spacecraft is now making a burn that drops the *Eagle* to within 50,000 feet of the Moon's surface. Neil Armstrong is looking out the window, carefully monitoring the landmarks below him.

**NARRATOR:**   4:05 P.M.

**REPORTER 3:**   A second burn has begun that is now positioning the *Eagle* away from the Moon.

**NARRATOR:**   4:08 P.M.

**REPORTER 1:**   Neil Armstrong is now repositioning the spacecraft into a face-up position. He and Aldrin are now flying with their backs to the Moon's surface.

**NARRATOR:**   4:10 P.M.

**REPORTER 2:**   The Eagle is now at 6,000 feet. (*excited*) Wait! Two warning lights have just gone off. Wait! Okay, okay. Mission Control has just given the go-ahead to ignore the lights. The mission can continue on track.

**NARRATOR:**   4:13 P.M.

**REPORTER 3:**   The on-board computer has just positioned the *Eagle* in an upright position. Armstrong can clearly see the intended landing site. It's a field of boulders in a crater. The *Eagle* has just enough fuel for five more minutes of flight.

**NARRATOR:**   4:15 P.M.

**REPORTER 1:**   Neil Armstrong has just made a decision to abandon the original landing site.

**NARRATOR:**   4:17 P.M.

**REPORTER 2:**   Armstrong has switched to manual control and has now flown over the crater. He is now slowing his rate of descent from about 20 feet per second to 3 feet per second.

**NARRATOR:**   4:18 P.M.

**REPORTER 3:**   Armstrong is now 1,100 feet west of the crater and is descending to a new landing spot.

**REPORTER 1:**   Now they're at 100 feet.

**REPORTER 2:**   75 feet.

**REPORTER 3:**   50 feet.

**NARRATOR:**   4:19 P.M.

**REPORTER 1:**   25 feet.

**REPORTER 2:**   15 feet.

**REPORTER 3:**   10 feet.

**REPORTER 1:**   5 feet.

**OFFSTAGE**
**VOICE:**   The Eagle has landed.

**NARRATOR:**   10:56 P.M.

**REPORTER 2:**   Neil Armstrong is crawling out of the Eagle feet first. He is descending the ladder.

**REPORTER 3:**   Armstrong has jumped down to the footpad, just a couple of inches from the surface of the Moon.

**REPORTER 1:**   Neil Armstrong is stepping out onto the Moon's surface—something no person has ever done before.

**OFFSTAGE**
**VOICE:**   That's one small step for man, one giant leap for mankind.

**NARRATOR:**   11:54 P.M.

**REPORTER 2:**   Armstrong and Aldrin are both walking on the Moon. During their walk they plant an American flag on the Moon's surface, gather nearly 50 pounds of Moon rocks, deploy three experiments, hammer some core tubes into the Moon's surface, and take many photographs.

**REPORTER 3:**   Both Aldrin and Armstrong have crawled back into the *Eagle.*

**NARRATOR:**   1:54 P.M. July 21.

**REPORTER 1:**   Twenty-one hours and 36 minutes after the *Eagle* landed on the surface of the Moon, the top half of the craft lifts the two astronauts off the surface of the Moon.

**REPORTER 2:**   The bottom half of the craft is left on the surface.

**NARRATOR:**   5:35 P.M.

**REPORTER 3:**   The *Eagle* has now reached an altitude of 60 miles above the Moon's surface and has now entered a lunar orbit.

**REPORTER 1:**   The *Eagle* has now come alongside *Columbia* and begins the docking procedure. Armstrong and Aldrin are now being reunited with Michael Collins who stayed aboard *Columbia.*

**REPORTER 2:**   The astronauts have now jettisoned the *Eagle*, the spacecraft that took them to and from the surface of Earth's satellite.

**NARRATOR:**   12:56 A.M.

**REPORTER 3:**   *Columbia* now begins the long trip back to Earth.

**NARRATOR:**   12:21 P.M, July 24, 1969.

**REPORTER 1:**   Eight days, three hours, eighteen minutes and thirty-five seconds after liftoff, the crew of *Apollo 11* splashes down safely into the Pacific Ocean.

**REPORTER 2:**   History has been made.

**REPORTER 3:**   Man has walked on the surface of the Moon.

**NARRATOR:**   This momentous trip was one of six successful landings on the surface of the Moon. During those voyages numerous scientific experiments were carried out and many new discoveries about our closest satellite were made. In all, about 882 pounds of Moon rocks were returned to the Earth for scientists to study. By the end of 1972, Project Apollo was concluded at a total cost of nearly $25 billion. Later space explorations focused on the development of space labs and space stations. These, too, will help further our understanding and appreciation of space.

[Note: The time sequences in this script have been taken from actual transcripts of the flight. The events reported are the actual events and have not been fictionalized.]

## Possible Extensions

1. Invite students to discuss the significance of the *Apollo 11* flight. How did it add to our knowledge about the Moon? Why was it so historic? What have we learned about the Moon in the years since that first manned landing?

2. Encourage students to imagine that they have landed on the surface of the Moon and have approximately 21 hours to spend any way they wish. What would they want to discover? What experiments would they want to perform? What would they want to see?

3. Invite small groups of students to each create a readers theatre script about the first manned landing on Mars. How would that landing be similar to or different from the first manned landing on the Moon?

4. Students may enjoy accessing additional information about the *Apollo 11* flight. The following Web sites can be particularly instructive:

   http://www.historyplace.com/unitedstates/apollo11/index.html

   http://www.nasm.edu/apollo/AS11/

   http://www.hq.nasa.gov/alsj/a11/images11.html

   http://www.nasm.edu/apollo30th/

5. Invite students to form two groups, one that supports the further exploration of space, one that argues against any further funding of space missions. Encourage students to discuss the funding of space missions versus the funding for social problems here at home. Which is more critical? Which is more important?

6. You may wish to share one or more of the following children's books with your students:

   *Apollo 11* by R. Conrad Stein (New York: Children's Press, 1992).

   *DK Discoveries: Moon Landing* by Carole Stott (New York: Dorling Kindersley, 1999).

   *First on the Moon: What It Was Like When Man Landed on the Moon* by Barbara Hehner (New York: Hyperion, 1999).

   *Man on the Moon* by Anastasia Suen (New York: Viking, 1997).

   *Race to the Moon: The Story of Apollo 11* by Jen Green (New York: Watts, 1998).

# Two Soldiers: Talking, Dying

## Staging

The narrator is off to the side and in the background in each scene. She/he can be placed at a lectern or podium. The characters move into position at the beginning of each scene (previous characters can exit as necessary).

### Scene 1

Narrator
X

    Leon        Carver       Larry      Thomas
     X           X           X         X

**NARRATOR:** It is 1968. The Vietnam War has escalated to the point that well over 500,000 American troops are fighting in this Southeast Asian country. Protests in the United States are at an all-time high. Thousands of people are demonstrating against the war, even as more and more troops are being sent overseas. It is a time of conflict and confrontation.

    As we look in on the first scene, we find two soldiers walking along a primitive dirt road in the Mekong Delta region of South Vietnam.

**140**

**CARVER:** Hey, guys, how are you doing?

**LARRY:** I'm doing just fine. But it sure is hot. (*wipes brow*) I don't like this heat. It's nothing like my hometown of Minneapolis. There it's just warm enough in the summer and cold enough in the winter. Just right, yes sir, just right. What about you, friend?

**THOMAS:** Well, because I'm from L.A., this heat doesn't bother me much. I guess I'm just a surfer boy at heart. Spent all my time on the beach, swimming and surfing the summer away. This heat isn't a problem for me. I guess I'm just used to it. I don't know about this humidity, though. It sure does make your clothes stick to you.

**LEON:** Yeah, Vietnam sure isn't like anything I've ever seen back in Oklahoma. Lots of jungles here; not like all the farmland where I live.

**CARVER:** Yeah, you're right. I'm used to the wide-open spaces of Pennsylvania. I couldn't ever imagine living in a country that was full of jungles.

**LARRY:** There are a lot of things this place isn't, but I sure don't want to go into that long list right . . .

(The sounds of gunfire and bombs [tapping on a drum, popping paper bags, banging on a table] are heard. The confusion of many voices screaming and yelling [members of the audience] builds and then dies away.)

## *Scene 2*

Narrator

  X

                Carver      Larry

                  X         X

**NARRATOR:** Carver and Larry have just endured a crushing hail of gunfire and bombing from the North Vietnamese. Their two friends, Leon and Thomas, are dead. Around them lay other dead and wounded members of their outfit. There is

a brief lull in the fighting while they wait for reinforce-
ments, as well as the medevac helicopters that will remove
them to distant field hospitals.

**CARVER:** (*desperate and crying*) Help me, help me, Larry. Man, I'm
all shot up. I can't feel anything in my legs. I can't move my
arm. I've got blood all over me. I'm dying, man, I'm dying.

**LARRY:** (*reassuringly*) Hold on, buddy, I'm right here. I'm not going
to leave you. Hey, that's what buddies are all about. You
just gotta hold on. The choppers will be here soon. Just
hold on a little longer.

**CARVER:** (*panicked*) I'm all shot up, man, I'm all shot up! Man, they
shot off my legs. THEY SHOT OFF MY LEGS!!

**LARRY:** Hey, pal, just calm down. You look a lot worse than you
are. Hey, that's just some of my blood on your shirt. Look
here, see, a stray bullet probably just ripped through my
arm here and I got blood flying all over the place. You just
got some on you, that's all.

**CARVER:** Man, I'm dying, I tell you, I'm dying. Don't let me die. Don't
let me die.

**LARRY:** (*insistent*) You're not going to die. You hear me! You're not
going to die. Hey, remember, I'm your friend and friends
don't tell other friends lies. Would I ever lie to you, man?

**CARVER:** No, you'd never lie to me. I'm just scared, that's all. I'm just
scared.

**LARRY:** We're all scared, man. I'm scared, you're scared, every
darned person in this unit is scared. Even Lieutenant
Mitchell is scared. If we weren't scared, we'd be dead.

**CARVER:** (*confused*) Why did this happen to me? WHY? Man, I was
just a happy little farmer boy from Pennsylvania working
on my parent's farm. Raising some pigs, taking care of
cornfields, and fixing tractors. I was happy, I was having a
good time, and then this stupid, stupid war had to come
along and mess everything up.

**LARRY:**   Hey, me too, pal. I had just taken a year off from college to "do my own thing." I was cruising up and down the California coast, living on the beach, surfin' whenever the waves were right, and having a grand time. Yeah, and then I get this notice from my folks that I've been drafted. Boy, was I ticked! Really messed up my life. I knew what was coming. After basic training it was right on to 'Nam. It was right on to a year of being shot at, being yelled at, and being bitten by a thousand and one animals I never heard of before. What a waste!

**CARVER:**   (*almost delirious*) Man, I'm dying . . . I'm dying. Hang on to me Lar, hang on.

**LARRY:**   I'm here, buddy, I'm here.

**CARVER:**   (*loudly*) Oh, man, I'm hurtin'. I'm really hurtin'. I don't know how much longer I can last.

(The sound of helicopters is heard in the distance [a sound effects recording can be used or several students can imitate the whirring of helicopter blades])

## Scene 3

Narrator
   X

|  | Carver | Nurse | Richard | Tyrone |
|---|---|---|---|---|
|  | X | X | X | X |

**NARRATOR:**   This next scene takes place in a hospital ward in Saigon. It is filled with soldiers with varying injuries—some minor and some major. One soldier, Richard, has a bandage around his head; another, Tyrone, has both arms in casts; and still others are missing limbs, have patches across both eyes, or are in various states of misery and pain. Nurses and doctors are everywhere, helping those who need it most and trying to calm those who are confused or may be dying. As we look in on this scene, Carver is in a hospital bed.

**CARVER:**  Hey, Nurse, do me a favor, will ya?

**NURSE:**  Sure, anything. Just name it.

**CARVER:**  Look. (he pulls a photo out of his shirt pocket) Here's my girl, you know the one I've been tellin' you about.

**NURSE:**  Yeah, you've done nothing but talk about Cindy, or "Cinderella" as you like to call her, ever since we you got to this hospital. She sure is pretty.

**CARVER:**  Would you believe that she was the prettiest girl in the whole high school? Yeah, every guy in the world wanted to take her out. But, you know what? She'd only go out with me. Yeah, out of all the jocks in the whole school she picked me.

**RICHARD:**  I don't understand how a girl that pretty would pick a guy as ugly as you. Either she had her eyes closed the whole time or she's even crazier than you are.

**CARVER:**  Nah, she just had good taste. And you know what, after this whole mess is over with I'm going right back to York County and ask her to marry me. Yes, my friends, you're lookin' at a picture of the future Mrs. Anderson.

**TYRONE:**  (*chuckling*) Yes, I can see it now. They'll make a movie of your lives and call it *Beauty and the Beast*.

**CARVER:**  Yeah, a lot you know. But, Nurse, I still need that favor.

**NURSE:**  Just name it.

**CARVER:**  If I don't make it out of this whole mess, I mean if they have to haul me outta here in a body bag I want you to do something for me. I want you to take these (he pulls off a set of "dog tags" from around his neck and hands them to the nurse) and send them to Cindy. And tell her that I love her. (*now in very severe pain*) You'll do that for me, won't you, won't you?

**NURSE:**  Consider it done.

**CARVER:**   (*labored and slow*) Man, I'm hurting. I'm really hurting.

**NURSE:**   I'm right here, Carver, I'm right here.

**CARVER:**   Darn war, why'd it ever have to happen? Why'd it ever have to happen?

**RICHARD:**   I sure don't know. Seems a shame that we're fighting this war and all those college kids back home are just marching in the streets or lying around some college campus.

**TYRONE:**   Yeah, here we are fighting our heads off and those college guys are protesting the war and marching up and down the streets burning their draft cards and all that stuff. We're the ones who are taking all the heat.

**CARVER:**   Oh, man, I'm hurting.

**NURSE:**   I'm still here, Carver, I'm still here. Although I'm not sure why I'm here. I always wanted to be a nurse, always wanted to help people. I was finishing nursing school back in Oregon when they needed some volunteers. So what did I do? I volunteered and before I knew it they sent me over here. Don't get me wrong, I'm glad to serve my country, glad to help out guys such as yourselves, but I just can't stand all the pain in here. Boys, good boys like yourselves, taking so much pain. I've never seen so much pain in one place before. They never told us about this back in nursing school. They never told us . . .

**CARVER:**   Nurse! Nurse!

**NURSE:**   What is it?

**CARVER:**   (*desperate*) Stay close to me. Don't leave me. Don't forget what I asked you to do. I'm hurting and I don't know what to do.

**NURSE:**   I won't leave. I'm right here. Hey, why don't you tell me some more about that girl of yours. Tell me some more about Cindy. I'm right here and I'm listening.

**NARRATOR:**   By 1968 more than 500,000 American soldiers were fighting in Vietnam. Many people supported the war because they believed that the fighting would stop the spread of Communism in this part of the world. Others opposed the war because too many soldiers were being killed and too much money was being spent on the conflict. Anti-war sentiments in the United States grew and many marches and anti-war rallies were staged in various parts of the country. Peace talks between the United States and North Vietnam took place in Paris between August 1969 and October 1971. A final agreement was reached in January 1973, and the United States began to withdraw its remaining troops from South Vietnam. In April 1975 the last Americans left Vietnam. During the conflict more than 55,000 Americans lost their lives in the war with many more permanently injured. The wounds of that war are still being felt today.

## Possible Extensions

1. Invite small groups of students to each write a fictitious letter from "Nurse" to "Cindy." What would she say about Carver? What information should she convey to Carver's girlfriend?

2. Invite students to access information on the events from 1960 to 1967 that led to the United States's involvement in Vietnam. Encourage students to construct a timeline of those events.

3. Invite students to read *The Wall* by Eve Bunting (New York: Clarion, 1990). Plan time to discuss the issues and concerns raised by this poignant and compelling book. Students may also wish to log on to the Web site about the Vietnam Veteran's Memorial: http://www.nps.gov/vive/index2.htm.

4. Students may wish to develop their own readers theatre script about the Vietnam War. They may wish to focus on the events happening in the United States during the time of the war (protests, confrontations, political scenarios, etc.).

5. Invite students to log on to one or more of the following Web sites, which present complete and thorough information about the Vietnam conflict:

   http://www.pbs.org/wgbh/amex/vietnam/

   http://www.pbs.org/battlefieldvietnam/

# Equal Rights Amendment

## Staging

The narrator can be standing off to the side of the staging area. Each of the other characters can also be standing or milling about the staging area as the story is unfolding.

| Angela | Carlo | Mara |
|--------|-------|------|
| X | X | X |

| Andrew | Curtis | Ramona |
|--------|--------|--------|
| X | X | X |

| T.J. | Brian | Jennifer |
|------|-------|----------|
| X | X | X |

Narrator
X

**NARRATOR:** In the 1960s and 1970s America was changing in many different ways. Real income of many American rose as poverty declined. Corporations grew and merged with each other. Universities expanded. Older Americans settled into special communities known as retirement towns. The

**147**

physical condition of most Americans was improving dramatically. But, perhaps, one of the most significant changes was the inclusion of more women into previously male-dominated areas of American life. Let's listen in to a conversation of high school students that could be taking place in a shopping mall or the corridor of any high school in the country.

**ANGELA:** (*proudly*) Hey, did you hear about the Equal Rights Amendment? It says, "Equality of rights under the law shall not be denied or abridged by the United States or by any state on account of sex."

**BRIAN:** What exactly does that mean?

**CARLO:** It means that in job hiring practices, sports, or other areas of our society women cannot be denied the same privileges and rights that men have.

**MARA:** I'm not so sure I'm in favor of this Equal Rights Amendment. I mean, as a woman, I'm perfectly content with my life. I can go to any school I want, I can live wherever I want, I can get any kind of job I want.

**ANDREW:** Yeah, I guess you're right. But, think about this: What if you were applying for a job and you and another person, a man, were equally qualified? And what if you were told that you couldn't have the job simply because you are female?

**ANGELA:** Well, I guess I would be pretty irritated. I mean, if we both had the same qualifications or skills, why shouldn't I have just as much right to that job as a man?

**CURTIS:** I think that's what the Equal Rights Amendment is trying to do. Personally, I think its a great idea. It's about time that women in this country had the same rights that men have.

**RAMONA:** I disagree. After all, things are okay just as they are. And, besides, the Equal Rights Amendment will undermine family life as well as some other traditional values in

American society. It will be like saying to women that equal jobs and equal pay are more important than raising a family or keeping a household together.

**T.J.:** Whoa. Now, just wait a minute Ramona. Are you trying to tell us that a woman's place is in the home?

**RAMONA:** No, not at all. What I'm trying to say is that there are some traditional values that Americans believe in. It has been proven through numerous psychological studies that women are the best caregivers for children . . .

**BRIAN:** (*interrupting*) Hey, now there's a pretty chauvinistic viewpoint. What about the father's role?

**RAMONA:** Hey, I'm not denying a father's role in raising children. All I'm saying is that mothers have been the traditional providers of care for children, and that this Equal Rights Amendment will be pulling mothers out of the home and placing them into factories, stores, and other places in the workforce.

**JENNIFER:** I'm not so sure. I think the ERA can be a good thing for the country. It will help women who want to look for jobs. It won't necessarily mean more jobs for women but will just give women a fighting chance in getting those jobs and, just as important, keeping those jobs once they have them.

**MARA:** You know what, I tend to disagree with Jennifer. It's just too much change all at once. I think there are some other issues we need to deal with in this country.

**ANGELA:** You mean like the energy crisis?

**CARLO:** Or what about welfare reform?

**ANDREW:** Or the economy?

**CURTIS:** Or law and order?

**T.J.:**   Yeah, you guys are right. There are many issues we need to think about. I'm just wondering if this ERA issue is one of the major ones our country should be working on.

**JENNIFER:**   Hey, think about it—women and men, equal rights, equal responsibilities, and equal guarantees.

**NARRATOR:**   The Equal Rights Amendment proposed complete equality before the law for both men and women. However, there were many who opposed the amendment, men and woman alike. Nevertheless, Congress passed it in 1972. Now it needed to be ratified by the states before it could become part of the U.S. Constitution. Many states argued the merits of this Amendment. Some voted to accept it, while others voted to reject it. In the end, 35 states ratified the Amendment by the July 1982 deadline. The Amendment needed 38 states to ratify it before it could become part of the Constitution. Other laws, however, have been passed that have provided women (and girls) with rights in the workforce as well as in sports.

# Possible Extensions ━━━━━━━━━━━━━━━━━━━━

1. Invite students to discuss the relative merits of the Equal Rights Amendment. You may wish to divide your class into two groups: those for the Amendment and those opposed to the Amendment. Encourage students to plan a debate on whether the Amendment should become a part of the U.S. Constitution.

2. Invite several professional women from the local community to visit your classroom and discuss their feelings about the ERA. How would their lives have changed if the ERA had been ratified and included within the Constitution?

3. Invite students to investigate the biographies of selected leaders in the ERA movement. What motivated those individuals? Where are those people today? How did their efforts influence any current or pending legislation?

4. Here are some related Web sites that your students may be interested in checking out:

    http://www.now.org/issues/economic/eratext.html

    http://www.now.org/issues/economic/cea/who.html

    http://www.equalrightsamendment.org

    http://www.gate.net/~liz/suffrage/eracom.htm

5. Here are a few books your students may enjoy reading:

    *Equality of the Sexes* by Emma Haughton (New York: Watts, 1997).

    *The Rights of Women and Girls* by Kary Moss (New York: Puffin, 1998).

    *Women Suffragists* by Diana Helmer (New York: Facts on File, 1998).

# Air to Breathe, Water to Drink

## Staging

All four characters can be standing or (preferably) walking around as they might do on a city sidewalk. The interviewer should have a homemade microphone in her or his hand as each character is interviewed. The narrator is off to the side of the staging area.

[Note: This script is open ended. You may wish to write the concluding remarks (by the child) or invite selected students to write those remarks prior to a performance.]

Narrator
  X

| Interviewer | Man | Woman | College Student | Child |
|---|---|---|---|---|
| X | X | X | X | X |

**NARRATOR:** How we care for the Earth and its inhabitants today will have a big impact on the world we live in tomorrow. We are now faced with many problems that affect the way we live and the ways in which our plants and our animal friends live, too. Air and water pollution, toxins and trash, and the destruction of the ozone layer (which filters out the harmful rays of the sun) may someday threaten all our lives.

152

These problems are not simple ones, and they require more than simple solutions. Unfortunately, some people don't realize the dangers we live with or don't care about the world we live in.

Let's listen in as our correspondent asks people on the street about this concern and what they can do about it.

**INTERVIEWER:** Excuse me, sir. I'd like to ask you a question.

**MAN:** Go ahead.

**INTERVIEWER:** Sir, it has been said that this country is in serious trouble, that is, as far as the environment is concerned. Do you agree with that statement?

**MAN:** No, not really. Look, I run a factory down by the river. I have more than 160 people working for me in that factory. That factory provides jobs for the people who work there. That factory pays taxes regularly and helps support the local economy. That factory produces goods that are purchased by people all over the country. Look at all the jobs, money, and taxes that come out of my factory. We're important to the community. The community needs us. Look at all we do. Just look.

**INTERVIEWER:** So, I guess what you're saying is that your factory isn't part of the problem, is that right?

**MAN:** Yeah, that's right. We're not the enemy here. We've created some good jobs. People are able to work and provide for their families because of my factory. People are able to have houses and cars and take vacations because of this factory. Without this factory, people would be out of work. Is that what you want, people out of work?

**INTERVIEWER:** Sir, it seems as though you're not concerned with the environmental impact of your factory.

**MAN:** That's not it at all. Of course, I'm concerned. But I've got to run a factory. I just don't have time for the environment.

**INTERVIEWER:** Thank you for your time, sir. (*turning to the woman*) Excuse me, may I please interview you for a few minutes?

**WOMAN:** Sure.

**INTERVIEWER:** Do you think that the environment is in danger?

**WOMAN:** Yes I do! I'm upset that factories are pouring dangerous chemicals into rivers and that the government isn't doing enough to clean up toxic waste sites. I'm upset that there is an enormous hole in the ozone layer that is growing larger every year. Sure, I think that the environment is in danger

**INTERVIEWER:** You seem to be quite passionate. Why?

**WOMAN:** I'm concerned about my children and about my children's children. What kind of world will they inherit? What kind of world will this be if we keeping dumping our trash or refuse to engage in recycling efforts. I'm just a little afraid of what this country will look like in 20 or 50 years.

**INTERVIEWER:** What are you doing to deal with this issue?

**WOMAN:** My family and I recycle. We regularly separate our organic and non-organic wastes. We maintain a compost pile in the backyard, which we use for our garden—an organic garden mind you. We restrict our use of electricity. We use the family car as little as possible, often combining several errands into one to save on gasoline. In fact, we do everything we possibly can to be environmentally conscious.

**INTERVIEWER:** You seem to put your beliefs into action.

**WOMAN:** We're trying our best. We're also trying to share our beliefs with our neighbors. We want them to practice some of the same things we do. It may not seem like much, but if everybody did just a little bit, perhaps, together, we could all make a big difference.

**INTERVIEWER:** Thank you. Excuse me. (*turns to the college student*) Would you mind being interviewed for a few minutes?

**STUDENT:** No, fire away.

**INTERVIEWER:** Some people are saying that our water supply is being polluted and that the air is being filled with dangerous chemicals. What do you think?

**STUDENT:** I really don't know. I'm just trying to make it through school so that I can get a job.

**INTERVIEWER:** You don't seem to care.

**STUDENT:** Of course I care, but I don't know what to do. I've read the articles in the local newspaper and in some news magazines. I've seen some stuff on the Internet. Yeah, there are some real issues out there. I'm just not sure how I can get involved. My time is pretty much taken up with my education and all. I've got research to do, papers to write, tests to take, classes to go to, and a part-time job at nights so I can pay for my education. Yeah, I wish I could get involved more, but I'm just not sure how.

**INTERVIEWER:** It seems like you're saying that the environment is just not that important to you.

**STUDENT:** It's not that, man. It's just that I'm not sure what I can do.

**INTERVIEWER:** Thank you. (*turns to child*) Excuse me, may I interview you?

**CHILD:** Sure.

**INTERVIEWER:** You've heard what everyone else has said. What do you think?

**CHILD:** _____

_____

_____

_____

**INTERVIEWER:** Why do you say that?

**CHILD:** _____

_____

_____

_____

**INTERVIEWER:** And, what do you think is our biggest environmental concern today?

**CHILD:** _____

_____

_____

_____

**INTERVIEWER:** And how can we deal with it?

**CHILD:** _____

_____

_____

_____

**INTERVIEWER:** What would you like to say to all the adults?

**CHILD:** _____

_____

_____

_____

**NARRATOR:** Preserving nature won't be easy. It will take lots of planning, energy, and people working together to ensure a natural and healthy life for ourselves and for all life on Earth. The time to start is now and the people to do the job are right here in this room—you and me!

# Possible Extensions

1. Provide multiple copies of this script to several different groups of students to craft their own ending to the play. Invite each group to perform their version of the script. Plan time afterwards to discuss the different endings and what they mean.

2. Invite students to share this script with their parents. Students may wish to interview their parents about their views or insights on environmental concerns. Plan time to share those viewpoints in class.

3. Encourage students to talk with school administrators or the custodial staff about any environmental concerns in and around the school. How are those concerns similar to or different from those in the larger community, county, or state?

4. Invite students to write "Letters to the Editor" of the local newspaper about specific environmental concerns in their local community or state.

5. Divide the class into several small groups. Invite each group to make a prediction about what the local community will look like in 10 years, 25 years, 100 years, and 1,000 years. What will be some of the environmental concerns of the future ? How can students work towards reducing or eliminating those concerns today?

6. Here are a few books (among many) that you may wish to share with your students:

    *Earth Science Book: Activities for Kids* by Dinah Zike (New York: John Wiley, 1993).

    *Exploring the Rainforest: Science Activities for Kids* by Anthony D. Fredericks (Golden, CO: Fulcrum Publishing, 1996).

    *50 Simple Things Kids Can Do to Save the Earth* by John Javna (Kansas City, KS: Andrews and McMeel, 1990).

    *Taking Care of the Earth: Kids in Action* by Laurence Pringle (Honesdale, PA: Boyds Mills Press, 1996).

    *Working in the Environment* by Corinna Nelson (Minneapolis, MN: Lerner, 1998).

# What's Ahead?

## Staging

There are no characters in this script. The students all play themselves. Invite the selected "performers" to pencil in their names on the appropriate blank lines below. There are also several "blanks" inserted throughout the script that are intended for students to complete (as part of an initial writing activity or "on the spot" as the script is being read). Many of the blanks will depend on recent historical events in the lives of the students, while other blanks will include historical events from many years in the past.

There is no narrator for this script. Students can be seated on chairs (as they would be in a classroom setting) or can be milling around (as they would be on the playground or at a mall).

1:_____ 2:_____
X X

3:_____ 4:_____
X X

5:_____ 6:_____
X X

**1:** Hey, guys. We're just about to graduate. What do you think is going to happen to us now?

**2:** I don't know. We're done with school and now we have to go out into the big, wide world and try to make it on our own.

**3:** I don't know about you guys, but I'm a little scared.

**4:** Yeah, me too. Like, what are we supposed to do?

**5:** Beats me. We read all those books, did all those lessons, and wrote all those papers in school. Now what?

**6:** Yeah, now what?

**1:** Well, remember what our history teacher said? You know, it was something like, "History has a way of repeating itself."

**2:** Boy, that's scary. Just look at what's happened in our lifetimes.

**3:** Yeah, there was the _____

_____

_____

**4:** And remember when the president _____

_____

_____

**5:** And who can forget when _____

_____

_____

**6:** The thing I'll remember most is when _____

_____

_____

**1:**  That's just like the time when _____

_____

_____

**2:**  Boy, even though we're only about _____ years old there's sure been a lot of stuff that's happened. I wonder what it all means?

**3:**  I guess kids our age wonder about stuff all the time. I bet kids back in the eleventh century worried about _____

_____

_____

**4:**  Yeah, and what about kids during the Revolutionary War? They probably thought a lot about _____

_____

_____

**5:**  Hey, that's nothing. How would you have liked to have been on a wagon train headed west in the 1800s? What do you think you would have done about _____

_____

_____

**6:**  Or what about those kids who had to fight in the Civil War? Do you guys think you could have _____

_____

_____

**1:**  I know one thing. I wouldn't have wanted to work in those sweat shops during the Industrial Revolution. Can you imagine _____

_____

_____

**2:**  Not me! What about all those people who lived during the Great Depression? All they could do was _____

_____

_____

_____

**3:**  And just think about all those guys at Pearl Harbor on December 7, 1941. That must have been totally scary when

_____

_____

_____

**4:**  Hey, talk about brave. What about those civil rights marches in the '60s? Do you guys think you could have

_____

_____

_____

**5:**  I know one thing, I sure wouldn't have wanted to be in Vietnam. I mean every day they just _____

_____

_____

_____

**6:**  Hey, don't forget what happened in the last part of the twentieth century. Remember when computers became the hottest thing around? I mean, before computers people couldn't even _____

_____

_____

_____

**1:**  Yeah, now computers can _____

_____

_____

**2:**  And here we are today. I still don't know what's going to happen in the future. I mean, does history really repeat itself? Will we see some of the same things next year or next century that we've seen already? I don't know. What do you guys think?

**3:**  I think that _____

_____

_____

**4:**  I think the most important historical event will be _____

_____

_____

_____

**5:**  I think it will be _____

_____

_____

**6:**  Yeah, maybe. But I really think we're going to be spending a lot of time _____

_____

_____

_____

**1:**  Yeah, and we'll also _____

_____

_____

_____

**2:** You know what? I think the most important historical event in our lifetimes will be _____

_____

_____

**3:** Hey! What would kids 500 years ago have thought about that?

**4:** What about kids 100 years ago?

**5:** What about kids 10 years ago?

**6:** I don't know about you guys. But I think that there's an awful lot to look forward to in our lifetimes. Yeah, an awful lot to look forward to.

## Possible Extensions

1. Invite students to complete the blanks and perform the script for another class. Encourage the two classes to engage in an active dialogue about their predictions and projections for the future.

2. Encourage students to provide a copy of this script to several adults and to invite them to fill in the appropriate blanks. Students can then perform the readers theatre script and discuss the adult's projections.

3. Invite students to substitute the names of several historical figures in place of their names. For example, if Leif Eriksson, Christopher Columbus, Thomas Jefferson, Abraham Lincoln, Martin Luther King Jr., and Neil Armstrong were used in place of the six student names how would the script change?

4. Invite students to videotape their performance of this script. Place the videotaped recording in a safe place and invite students to return in a year to view their performance. How accurate were their predictions? What would they want to change about their predictions?

5. Invite each student to write a prediction about a major historical event that might happen in the next five years. Place each prediction in a separate self-addressed, stamped envelope and store them in a safe location. Mail the envelopes to the students in five years. Invite students to write back and share their thoughts about the accuracy of their predictions.

# Resources

## Books About Readers Theatre

Braun, W., and C. Braun. *Readers Theatre: Scripted Rhymes and Rhythms*. Calgary, AB, Canada: Braun and Braun Educational Enterprises, 1995.

Coger, L. I., and M. R. White. *Readers Theatre Handbook: A Dramatic Approach to Literature*. Glenview, IL: Scott, Foresman, 1982.

Dixon, N., A. Davies, and C. Politano. *Learning with Readers Theatre: Building Connections*. Winnipeg, MB, Canada: Peguis, 1996.

Hill, S. *Readers Theatre: Performing the Text*. Armadale, Australia: Eleanor Curtain, 1990.

Johnson, T. D., and D. R. Louis. *Bringing It All Together: A Program for Literacy*. Portsmouth, NH: Heinemann, 1990.

Plant, R. *Readers Theatre in the Elementary Classroom: A Take Part Teacher's Guide*. North Vancouver, BC, Canada: Take Part Productions, 1990.

Shepard, A. *Stories on Stage: Scripts for Reader's Theater*. New York: H. W. Wilson, 1993.

Sloyer, S. *Readers Theatre: Story Dramatization in the Classroom*. Urbana, IL: National Council for Teachers of English, 1982.

Tanner, F. *Creative Communication: Projects in Acting, Speaking, Oral Reading*. Pocatello, ID: Clark, 1979.

——. *Readers Theatre Fundamentals*. Pocatello, ID: Clark, 1993.

# Sources for Additional Readers Theatre Scripts

Barchers, S. *Fifty Fabulous Fables: Beginning Readers Theatre*. Englewood, CO: Teacher Ideas Press, 1997.

———. *Muticultural Folktales: Readers Theatre for Elementary Students*. Englewood, CO: Teacher Ideas Press, 2000.

———. *Readers Theatre for Beginning Readers*. Englewood, CO: Teacher Ideas Press, 1993.

———. *Scary Readers Theatre*. Englewood, CO: Teacher Ideas Press, 1994.

Criscoe, B. L., and P. J. Lanasa. *Fairy Tales for Two Readers*. Englewood, CO: Teacher Ideas Press, 1995.

Fredericks, A. D. *Frantic Frogs and Other Frankly Fractured Folktales for Readers Theatre*. Englewood, CO: Teacher Ideas Press, 1993.

———. *Silly Salamanders and Other Slightly Stupid Stories for Readers Theatre*. Englewood, CO: Teacher Ideas Press, 2000.

———. *Tadpole Tales and Other Totally Terrific Treats for Readers Theatre*. Englewood, CO: Teacher Ideas Press, 1997.

Georges, C., and C. Cornett. *Reader's Theatre*. Buffalo, NY: D.O.K. Publishers, 1990.

Haven, K. *Great Moments in Science: Experiments and Readers Theatre*. Englewood, CO: Teacher Ideas Press, 1996.

Latrobe, K. H., C. Casey, and L. A. Gann. *Social Studies Readers Theatre for Young Adults*. Englewood, CO: Teacher Ideas Press, 1991.

Latrobe, K. H., and M. K. Laughlin. *Readers Theatre for Young Adults*. Englewood, CO: Teacher Ideas Press, 1989.

Laughlin, M. K., and K. H. Latrobe. *Readers Theatre for Children*. Englewood, CO: Teacher Ideas Press, 1990.

Laughlin, M. K., P. T. Black, and K. H. Latrobe. *Social Studies Readers Theatre for Children*. Englewood, CO: Teacher Ideas Press, 1991.

Pfeffinger, C. R. *Holiday Readers Theatre*. Englewood, CO: Teacher Ideas Press, 1994.

# Web Sites

http://www.aaronshep.com/rt/index.html
How to use readers theatre, sample scripts from a children's author who specializes in readers theatre, and an extensive list of resources.

http://falcon.jmu.edu/~ramseyil/drama.htm
Links for storytelling, creative dramatics, puppetry and readers theatre for children and young adults highlight this site.

http://mcrel.org/resources/plus/theatre.html
Lesson plan activities, teacher's guides, how to adapt stories to a readers theatre format, and online children's stories.

http://www.readerstheatre.com
An organization dedicated to the development and use of readers theatre in education.

http://www.geocities.com/EnchantedForest/Tower/3235/index.html
This is a download page for the "RT Script Pack," a set of readers theatre scripts in Microsoft Word format. Reading levels vary from beginner to adult.

http://www.loiswalker.com/catalog/
Lots of readers theatre scripts for a variety of reading levels and ages.

http://www.storycart.com
Storycart Press's subscription service provides an inexpensive opportunity to have timely scripts delivered to teachers each month. Each script is created or adapted by well-known writer Suzanne Barchers, author of several readers theatre books (see above).

# Professional Organizations

Readers Theatre International
Box 40
Brentwood Bay
British Columbia, Canada
V8M IR3
(250) 544-1162
http://www.readerstheatre.com

Institute for Readers Theatre
P.O. Box 178333
San Diego, CA 92177
(858) 276-1848
http://www.readers-theatre.com

# More Teacher Resources
## by Anthony D. Fredericks

All of the following books are available from Teacher Ideas Press (P.O. Box 6633, Englewood, CO 80155); 1-800-237-6124; http://www.lu.com/tip.

*Frantic Frogs and Other Frankly Fractured Folktales for Readers Theatre* [ISBN: 1-56308-174-1]. (123 pages; $19.50)

Have you heard "Don't Kiss Sleeping Beauty, She's Got Really Bad Breath" or "The Brussels Sprouts Man (The Gingerbread Man's Unbelievably Strange Cousin)"? This resource (grades 4–8) offers 30 reproducible satirical scripts for rip-roaring dramatics. Side-splitting send-ups and wacky folktales are guaranteed to bring snickers, chuckles, and belly laughs into the classroom.

*The Integrated Curriculum: Books for Reluctant Readers, Grades 2–5* (2d Edition) [ISBN: 0-87287-994-1]. (220 pages; $22.50)

This book presents guidelines for motivating and using literature with reluctant readers. It contains more than 40 book units on titles carefully selected to motivate the most reluctant readers, such as *The Three Bears*, *The Salamander Room*, and *Sky Tree*. Each unit includes a summary, discussion questions that foster critical thinking, and cross-curricular extensions.

*Involving Parents Through Children's Literature: P–K* [ISBN: 1-56308-022-2]. (86 pages; $15.00)

*Involving Parents Through Children's Literature: Grades 1–2* [ISBN: 1-56308-012-5]. (95 pages; $14.50)

*Involving Parents Through Children's Literature: Grades 3–4* [ISBN: 1-56308-013-3]. (96 pages; Out of print.)

*Involving Parents Through Children's Literature: Grades 5–6* [ISBN: 1-56308-014-1]. (107 pages; Out of print.)

This series of four books stimulates parent participation in the learning process. Reproducible activity sheets based on quality children's books are designed in a convenient format so children can take them home. Each sheet includes a book summary, discussion questions, and engaging activities for adults and children that stimulate comprehension and promote reading enjoyment.

*The Librarian's Complete Guide to Involving Parents Through Children's Literature: Grades K–6* [ISBN: 1-56308-538-0]. (137 pages; $24.50)

Activities for 101 children's books are presented in a reproducible format, so librarians can distribute them to students to take home and share with parents. Each sheet includes a book summary, discussion questions, and a list of learning activities for parents to do with their children. These projects build strong bonds of communication between parents and children.

*More Social Studies Through Children's Literature: An Integrated Approach* [ISBN: 1-56308-761-8]. (225 pages; $27.50)

Energize your social studies curriculum with dynamic, "hands-on, minds-on" projects based on such great children's books as *Amazing Grace*, *Fly Away Home*, and *Lon Po Po*. This book offers hundreds of activities designed to stimulate and engage students in positive learning and help teachers implement national (and many state) standards. Each of the 33 units has book summaries, social studies topic areas, critical thinking questions, and dozens of easy-to-do activities for every grade level. This book is a perfect compliment to the earlier *Social Studies Through Children's Literature: An Integrated Approach* and effectively builds upon the success of that volume.

*Readers Theatre for American History* [ISBN: 1-56308-860-6]. (234 pages; $30.00).

This book offers a participatory approach to American History. The 25 scripts stimulate students to become active participants in several historical events. Students will work alongside Father Junipero Serra at Mission San Juan Capistrano; they'll stand alongside Thomas Jefferson as he drafts the Declaration of Independence; they'll travel with a Midwestern family as they trek across the Oregon Trail; and they'll travel with Neal Armstrong in his history-making trip to the Moon. In short, students will get a "you are there" perspective to the unfolding of critical milestones and memorable circumstances that have shaped the American experience.

*Science Adventures with Children's Literature: A Thematic Approach* [ISBN: 1-56308-417-1]. (190 pages; $24.50)

Focusing on the new Science Education Standards, this activity-centered resource uses a wide variety of children's literature to integrate science across the elementary curriculum. With a thematic approach, it features the best in science trade books; stimulating "hands-on, minds-on" activities and experiments in life, physical, Earth, and space sciences; and a host of tips, ideas, and strategies that make teaching and learning science an adventure. A delightful array of creative suggestions, dynamic thematic units in all areas of science, and stimulating new science literature and activities highlight this resource.

*Science Discoveries on the Net: An Integrated Approach* [ISBN: 1-56308-823-1]. (315 pages; $27.50)

This book is designed to help teachers integrate the Internet into their science programs and enhance the scientific discoveries of students. The 88 units emphasize key concepts—based on national and state standards—throughout the science curriculum. Each unit is divided into five sections: Introduction (which include basic background information on a topic), Research Questions (for students to investigate), Web Sites (the most current Internet sites on a topic), Children's Literature (the best books about a subject), and Activities (a host of "hands-on, minds-on" projects). The units are designed to energize any science curriculum and any classroom program.

*Silly Salamanders and Other Slightly Stupid Stuff for Readers Theatre* [ISBN: 1-56308-825-8]. (161 pages; $23.50)

The third entry in the "wild and wacky" readers theatre trilogy is just as crazy and just as weird as the first two. How about these stories: "Snow White and the Seven Vertically Challenged Men," "The Big Bad Salamander and the Three Little Pigs," and "King Arthur and the Knights of the Polygon Table." This unbelievable resource offers students in grades 3–6 dozens of silly send-ups of well-known fairy tales, legends, and original stories guaranteed to fill any classroom with peels of laughter, howls of delight, and incredible language arts activities. It's a guaranteed winner!

*Social Studies Discoveries on the Net: An Integrated Approach* [ISBN: 1-56308-824-X]. (276 pages; $26.00)

This book is designed to help teachers integrate the Internet into their social studies programs and enhance the classroom discoveries of students. The 75 units emphasize key concepts—based on national and state standards—throughout the social studies curriculum. Each unit is divided into five sections: Introduction (which include basic background information on a topic), Research Questions (for students to investigate), Web Sites (the most current Internet sites on a topic), Children's Literature (the best books about a subject), and Activities (a host of "hands-on, minds-on" projects). The units are designed to energize any social studies curriculum and any classroom program.

*Social Studies Through Children's Literature: An Integrated Approach* [ISBN: 0-87287-970-4]. (192 pages; $24.00)

Each of the 32 instructional units contained in this resource uses an activity-centered approach to elementary social studies, featuring children's picture books such as *Ox-Cart Man, In Coal Country,* and *Jambo Means Hello.* Each unit contains a book summary, social studies topic areas, curricular perspectives, critical thinking questions, and a large section of activities.

*Tadpole Tales and Other Totally Terrific Titles for Readers Theatre* [ISBN: 1-56308-547-X]. (115 pages; $18.50)

A follow-up volume to the best-selling *Frantic Frogs and Other Frankly Fractured Folktales for Readers Theatre,* this book provides primary-level readers (grades 1–4) with a humorous assortment of wacky tales based on well-known Mother Goose rhymes. For example, "Old MacDonald Had a Farm and, Boy, Did It Stink (E-I-E-I-O)." More than 30 scripts and dozens of classroom extensions will keep your students rolling in the aisles.

# About the Author

Tony is a nationally recognized children's literature expert well known for his energetic, fast-paced, and highly practical presentations for strengthening elementary science education. His dynamic and stimulating seminars have captivated thousands of teachers from coast to coast and border to border—all with rave reviews! His background includes extensive experience as a classroom teacher, curriculum coordinator, staff developer, author, professional storyteller, and university specialist in children's literature and science education.

*Anthony D. Fredericks*

Tony has written more than 50 teacher resource books in a variety of areas, including the hilarious *Tadpole Tales and Other Totally Terrific Treats for Readers Theatre* (Teacher Ideas Press), the award-winning *The Complete Phonemic Awareness Handbook* (Rigby), the best-selling *The Complete Guide to Thematic Units: Creating the Integrated Curriculum* (Christopher-Gordon), the celebrated *The Complete Science Fair Handbook*, co-authored with Isaac Asimov (Pearson Learning), and the extremely funny *Silly Salamanders and Other Slightly Stupid Stuff for Readers Theatre* (Teacher Ideas Press).

Not only is Tony an advocate for the integration of children's literature throughout the elementary curriculum, he is also the author of more than 20 highly acclaimed children's books including *Exploring the Rainforest* (Fulcrum), *Slugs* (Lerner), *Cannibal Animals* (Watts), *Under One Rock* (Dawn), *Exploring the Oceans* (Fulcrum), and *Zebras* (Lerner). He is currently a professor of education at York College in York, Pennsylvania. There, he teaches elementary methods courses in reading, language arts, science, and social studies. Additionally, he maintains a children's author Web site at http://www.afredericks.com, which is specifically designed for classrooms and schools across the country.

from *Teacher Ideas Press*

## CELEBRATING THE EARTH: Stories, Experiences, Activities
*Norma J. Livo*

Invite young readers to observe, explore, and appreciate the natural world through engaging activities. Livo shows you how to use folk stories, personal narrative, and a variety of learning projects to teach students about amphibians, reptiles, mammals, constellations, plants, and other natural phenomena. Designed to build a Naturalist Intelligence in young learners, these stories and activities are packed with scientific information. **All Levels.**
*xvii, 174p. 8½x11 paper ISBN 1-56308-776-6*

## FAMOUS PROBLEMS AND THEIR MATHMATICIAN
*Art Johnson*

Why did ordering an omelet cost one mathematician his life? The answer to this and other questions are found in this exciting new resource that shows your students how 60 mathematicians discovered mathematical solutions through everyday situations. These lessons are easily incorporated into the curriculum as an introduction to a math concept, a homework piece, or an extra challenge. Teacher notes and suggestions for the classroom are followed by extension problems and additional background material. **Grades 5–12.**
*xvi, 179p. 8½x11 paper ISBN 1-56308-446-5*

## SCIENCE AND MATH BOOKMARK BOOK: 300 Fascinating, Fact-Filled Bookmarks
*Kendall Haven and Roni Berg*

Use these 300 reproducible bookmarks of fascinating facts, concepts, trivia, inventions, and discoveries to spark student learning. They cover all major disciplines of math and physical, earth, and life sciences—ready to copy, cut out, and give to your students. **Grades 4 and up.**
*xii, 115p. 8½x11 paper ISBN 1-56308-675-1*

## WRITE RIGHT! Creative Writing Using Storytelling Techniques
*Kendall Haven*

Haven's breakthrough approach to creative writing uses storytelling techniques to enhance the creative writing process. This practical guide offers you directions for 38 writing exercises that will show students how to create powerful and dynamic fiction. All the steps are included, from finding inspiration and creating believable characters to the final edit. Activities are coded by levels, but most can be adapted to various grades. **All Levels.**
*240p. 8½x11 paper ISBN 1-56308-677-8*

## VISUAL MESSAGES: Integrating Imagery into Instruction
2d Edition
*David M. Considine and Gail E. Haley*

The authors provide effective media literacy strategies, activities, and resources that help students learn the critical-viewing skills necessary in our media-dominated world. Various media and types of programs are addressed, including motion pictures, television news, and advertising. Activities are coded by grade level and curriculum area. **Grades K–12.**
*xxiii,371p. 8½x11 paper ISBN 1-56308-575-5*

*For a free catalog or to place an order, please contact:*
**Teacher Ideas Press**
Dept. B051 • P.O. Box 6633 • Englewood, CO • 80155-6633
800-237-6124 • www.lu.com/tip • Fax: 303-220-8843